THE
MACHINE
LEARNING
WORKSHOP

SECOND EDITION

Get ready to develop your own high-performance machine learning algorithms with scikit-learn

Hyatt Saleh

THE MACHINE LEARNING WORKSHOP
SECOND EDITION

Copyright © 2020 Packt Publishing

Author: Hyatt Saleh

Reviewers: John Wesley Doyle, Akshat Gupta, Harshil Jain, Vikraman Karunanidhi, Subhojit Mukherjee, Madhav Pandya, Aditya Rane, and Subhash Sundaravadivelu

Managing Editor: Rutuja Yerunkar

Acquisitions Editors: Manuraj Nair, Kunal Sawant, Sneha Shinde, Anindya Sil, and Karan Wadekar

Production Editor: Shantanu Zagade

Editorial Board: Megan Carlisle, Samuel Christa, Mahesh Dhyani, Heather Gopsill, Manasa Kumar, Alex Mazonowicz, Monesh Mirpuri, Bridget Neale, Dominic Pereira, Shiny Poojary, Abhishek Rane, Brendan Rodrigues, Erol Staveley, Ankita Thakur, Nitesh Thakur, and Jonathan Wray

First published: November 2018
Second edition: July 2020
Production reference: 1210720
ISBN: 978-1-83921-906-1
Published by Packt Publishing Ltd.
Livery Place, 35 Livery Street
Birmingham B3 2PB, UK

EXPERIENCE THE WORKSHOP ONLINE

Thank you for purchasing the print edition of *The Machine Learning Workshop, Second Edition*. Every physical print copy includes free online access to the premium interactive edition. There are no extra costs or hidden charges.

Figure A: An example of the companion video in the Workshop course player (dark mode)

With the interactive edition you'll unlock:

- **Screencasts**: Supercharge your progress with screencasts of all exercises and activities.

- **Built-In Discussions**: Engage in discussions where you can ask questions, share notes and interact. Tap straight into insight from expert instructors and editorial teams.

- **Skill Verification**: Complete the course online to earn a Packt credential that is easy to share and unique to you. All authenticated on the public Bitcoin blockchain.

- **Download PDF and EPUB**: Download a digital version of the course to read offline. Available as PDF or EPUB, and always DRM-free.

To redeem your free digital copy of *The Machine Learning Workshop, Second Edition,* you'll need to follow these simple steps:

1. Visit us at https://courses.packtpub.com/pages/redeem.

2. Login with your Packt account, or register as a new Packt user.

3. Select your course from the list, making a note of the three page numbers for your product. Your unique redemption code needs to match the order of the pages specified.

4. Open up your print copy and find the codes at the bottom of the pages specified. They'll always be in the same place:

EXERCISE 4.02: PERFORMING MISSING VALUE ANALYSIS FOR THE DATAFRAMES

In this section, we will be implementing a missing value analysis on the first DataFrame to find the missing values. This exercise is a continuation of *Exercise 4.01, Importing Data into DataFrames*. Follow these steps to complete this exercise:

1. Import the **missingno** package:

```
# To analyze the missing data
!pip install missingno
import missingno as msno
```

2. Find the missing values in the first DataFrame and visualize the missing values in a plot:

```
# Missing Values in the first DataFrame
msno.bar(dataframes[0],color='red',labels=True,sort="ascending")
```

A B 2 1 C

Figure B: Example code in the bottom-right corner, to be used for free digital redemption of a print workshop

5. Merge the codes together (without spaces), ensuring they are in the correct order.

6. At checkout, click **Have a redemption code?** and enter your unique product string. Click **Apply**, and the price should be free!

Finally, we'd like to thank you for purchasing the print edition of *The Machine Learning Workshop, Second Edition*! We hope that you finish the course feeling capable of tackling challenges in the real world. Remember that we're here to help if you ever feel like you're not making progress.

If you run into issues during redemption (or have any other feedback) you can reach us at workshops@packt.com.

Table of Contents

Chapter 2: Unsupervised Learning – Real-Life Applications   49

Chapter 3: Supervised Learning – Key Steps 89

Chapter 4: Supervised Learning Algorithms: Predicting Annual Income   125

Chapter 5: Supervised Learning – Key Steps   157

PREFACE

ABOUT THE BOOK

Machine learning algorithms are an integral part of almost all modern applications. To make the learning process faster and more accurate, you need a tool flexible and powerful enough to help you build machine learning algorithms quickly and easily. With *The Machine Learning Workshop, Second Edition*, you'll master the scikit-learn library and become proficient in developing clever machine learning algorithms.

The Machine Learning Workshop, Second Edition, begins by demonstrating how unsupervised and supervised learning algorithms work by analyzing a real-world dataset of wholesale customers. Once you've got to grips with the basics, you'll develop an artificial neural network using scikit-learn and then improve its performance by fine-tuning hyperparameters. Towards the end of the workshop, you'll study the dataset of a bank's marketing activities and build machine learning models that can list clients who are likely to subscribe to a term deposit. You'll also learn how to compare these models and select the optimal one.

By the end of *The Machine Learning Workshop, Second Edition*, you'll not only have learned the difference between supervised and unsupervised models and their applications in the real world, but you'll also have developed the skills required to get started with programming your very own machine learning algorithms.

AUDIENCE

The Machine Learning Workshop, Second Edition, is perfect for machine learning beginners. You will need Python programming experience, though no prior knowledge of scikit-learn and machine learning is necessary.

ABOUT THE CHAPTERS

Chapter 1, Introduction to Scikit-Learn, introduces the two main topics of the book: machine learning and scikit-learn. It explains the key steps of preprocessing your input data, separating the features from the target, dealing with messy data, and rescaling the values of data.

Chapter 2, Unsupervised Learning – Real-Life Applications, explains the concept of clustering in machine learning by covering the three most common clustering algorithms.

Chapter 3, Supervised Learning – Key Steps, describes the different tasks that can be solved through supervised learning algorithms: classification and regression.

Chapter 4, *Supervised Learning Algorithms: Predicting Annual Income*, teaches the different concepts and steps for solving a supervised learning data problem.

Chapter 5, *Artificial Neural Networks: Predicting Annual Income*, shows how to solve a supervised learning classification problem using a neural network and analyze the results by performing error analysis.

Chapter 6, *Building Your Own Program*, explains all the steps required to develop a comprehensive machine learning solution.

CONVENTIONS

Code words in text, database table names, folder names, filenames, file extensions, path names, dummy URLs, user input, and Twitter handles are shown as follows:

"Load the **titanic** dataset using the **seaborn** library."

Words that you see on the screen (for example, in menus or dialog boxes) appear in the same format.

A block of code is set as follows:

```
import seaborn as sns
titanic = sns.load_dataset('titanic')
titanic.head(10)
```

New terms and important words are shown like this:

"Data that is missing information or that contains outliers or noise is considered to be **messy data**."

CODE PRESENTATION

Lines of code that span multiple lines are split using a backslash (\ ). When the code is executed, Python will ignore the backslash, and treat the code on the next line as a direct continuation of the current line.

For example:

```
history = model.fit(X, y, epochs=100, batch_size=5, verbose=1, \
                    validation_split=0.2, shuffle=False)
```

Comments are added into code to help explain specific bits of logic. Single-line comments are denoted using the **#** symbol, as follows:

```
# Print the sizes of the dataset
print("Number of Examples in the Dataset = ", X.shape[0])
print("Number of Features for each example = ", X.shape[1])
```

Multi-line comments are enclosed by triple quotes, as shown below:

```
"""
Define a seed for the random number generator to ensure the
result will be reproducible
"""
seed = 1
np.random.seed(seed)
random.set_seed(seed)
```

SETTING UP YOUR ENVIRONMENT

Before we explore the book in detail, we need to set up specific software and tools. In the following section, we shall see how to do that.

INSTALLING PYTHON ON WINDOWS AND MACOS

Follow these steps to install Python 3.7 on Windows and macOS:

1. Visit https://www.python.org/downloads/release/python-376/ to download Python 3.7.

2. At the bottom of the page, locate the table under the heading **Files**:

    For Windows, click on **Windows x86-64 executable installer** for 64-bit or **Windows x86 executable installer** for 32-bit.

    For macOS, click on **macOS 64-bit/32-bit installer** for macOS 10.6 and later, or **macOS 64-bit installer** for macOS 10.9 and later.

3. Run the installer that you have downloaded.

INSTALLING PYTHON ON LINUX

1. Open your Terminal and type the following command:

    ```
    sudo apt-get install python3.7
    ```

INSTALLING PIP

pip is included by default with the installation of Python 3.7. However, it may be the case that it does not get installed. To check whether it was installed, execute the following command in your Terminal or Command Prompt:

```
pip --version
```

You might need to use the **pip3** command, due to previous versions of **pip** on your computer that are already using the **pip** command.

If the **pip** command (or **pip3**) is not recognized by your machine, follow these steps to install it:

1. To install **pip**, visit https://pip.pypa.io/en/stable/installing/ and download the **get-pip.py** file.

2. Then, on the Terminal or Command Prompt, use the following command to install it:

```
python get-pip.py
```

You might need to use the **python3 get-pip.py** command, due to previous versions of Python on your machine that are already using the **python** command.

INSTALLING LIBRARIES

pip comes pre-installed with Anaconda. Once Anaconda is installed on your machine, all the required libraries can be installed using **pip**, for example, **pip install numpy**. Alternatively, you can install all the required libraries using **pip install -r requirements.txt**. You can find the **requirements.txt** file at https://packt.live/2Ar1i3v.

The exercises and activities will be executed in Jupyter Notebooks. Jupyter is a Python library and can be installed in the same way as the other Python libraries – that is, with **pip install jupyter**, but fortunately, it comes pre-installed with Anaconda. To open a notebook, simply run the command **jupyter notebook** in the Terminal or Command Prompt.

OPENING A JUPYTER NOTEBOOK

1. Open a Terminal/Command Prompt.

2. In the Terminal/Command Prompt, go to the directory location where you have cloned the book's repository.

3. Open a Jupyter notebook by typing in the following command:

```
jupyter notebook
```

4. By executing the previous command, you will be able to use Jupyter notebooks through the default browser of your machine.

ACCESSING THE CODE FILES

You can find the complete code files of this book at https://packt.live/2wkiC8d. You can also run many activities and exercises directly in your web browser by using the interactive lab environment at https://packt.live/3cYbopv.

We've tried to support interactive versions of all activities and exercises, but we recommend a local installation as well for instances where this support isn't available.

The high-quality color images used in this book can be found at https://packt.live/3exaFfJ.

If you have any issues or questions about installation, please email us at workshops@packt.com.

1

INTRODUCTION TO SCIKIT-LEARN

OVERVIEW

This chapter introduces the two main topics of this book: machine learning and scikit-learn. By reading this book, you will learn about the concept and application of machine learning. You will also learn about the importance of data in machine learning, as well as the key aspects of data preprocessing to solve a variety of data problems. This chapter will also cover the basic syntax of scikit-learn. By the end of this chapter, you will have a firm understanding of scikit-learn's syntax so that you can solve simple data problems, which will be the starting point for developing machine learning solutions.

INTRODUCTION

Machine learning (**ML**), without a doubt, is one of the most relevant technologies nowadays as it aims to convert information (data) into knowledge that can be used to make informed decisions. In this chapter, you will learn about the different applications of ML in today's world, as well as the role that data plays. This will be the starting point for introducing different data problems throughout this book that you will be able to solve using scikit-learn.

Scikit-learn is a well-documented and easy-to-use library that facilitates the application of ML algorithms by using simple methods, which ultimately enables beginners to model data without the need for deep knowledge of the math behind the algorithms. Additionally, thanks to the ease of use of this library, it allows the user to implement different approximations (that is, create different models) for a data problem. Moreover, by removing the task of coding the algorithm, scikit-learn allows teams to focus their attention on analyzing the results of the model to arrive at crucial conclusions.

Spotify, a world-leading company in the field of music streaming, uses scikit-learn because it allows them to implement multiple models for a data problem, which are then easily connected to their existing development. This process improves the process of arriving at a useful model, while allowing the company to plug them into their current app with little effort.

On the other hand, booking.com uses scikit-learn due to the wide variety of algorithms that the library offers, which allows them to fulfill the different data analysis tasks that the company relies on, such as building recommendation engines, detecting fraudulent activities, and managing the customer service team.

Considering the preceding points, this chapter also explains scikit-learn and its main uses and advantages, and then moves on to provide a brief explanation of the scikit-learn **Application Programming Interface** (**API**) syntax and features. Additionally, the process of representing, visualizing, and normalizing data will be shown. The aforementioned information will help us to understand the different steps that need to be taken to develop a ML model.

In the following chapters in this book, you will explore the main ML algorithms that can be used to solve real-life data problems. You will also learn about different techniques that you can use to measure the performance of your algorithms and how to improve them accordingly. Finally, you will explore how to make use of a trained model by saving it, loading it, and creating APIs.

INTRODUCTION TO MACHINE LEARNING

Machine learning (**ML**) is a subset of **Artificial Intelligence** (**AI**) that consists of a wide variety of algorithms capable of learning from the data that is being fed to them, without being specifically programmed for a task. This ability to learn from data allows the algorithms to create models that are capable of solving complex data problems by finding patterns in historical data and improving them as new data is fed to the models.

These different ML algorithms use different approximations to solve a task (such as probability functions), but the key element is that they are able to consider a countless number of variables for a particular data problem, making the final model better at solving the task than humans are. The models that are created using ML algorithms are created to find patterns in the input data so that those patterns can be used to make informed predictions in the future.

APPLICATIONS OF ML

Some of the popular tasks that can be solved using ML algorithms are price/demand predictions, product/service recommendation, and data filtering, among others. The following is a list of real-life examples of such tasks:

- **On-demand price prediction**: Companies whose services vary in price according to demand can use ML algorithms to predict future demand and determine whether they will have the capability to meet it. For instance, in the transportation industry, if future demand is low (low season), the price for flights will drop. On the other hand, is demand is high (high season), flights are likely to increase in price.

- **Recommendations in entertainment**: Using the music that you currently use, as well as that of the people similar to you, ML algorithms can construct models capable of suggesting new records that you may like. That is also the case of video streaming applications, as well as online bookstores.

- **Email filtering**: ML has been used for a while now in the process of filtering incoming emails in order to separate spam from your desired emails. Lately, it also has the capability to sort unwanted emails into more categories, such as social and promotions.

CHOOSING THE RIGHT ML ALGORITHM

When it comes to developing ML solutions, it is important to highlight that, more often than not, there is no one solution for a data problem, much like there is no algorithm that fits all data problems. According to this and considering that there is a large quantity of algorithms in the field of ML, choosing the right one for a certain data problem is often the turning point that separates outstanding models from mediocre ones.

The following steps can help narrow down the algorithms to just a few:

1. **Understand your data**: Considering that data is the key to being able to develop any ML solutions, the first step should always be to understand it in order to be able to filter out any algorithm that is unable to process such data.

   For instance, considering the quantity of features and observations in your dataset, it is possible to determine whether an algorithm capable of producing outstanding results with a small dataset is required. The number of instances/features to consider a dataset small depends on the data problem, the quantity of the outputs, and so on. Moreover, by understanding the types of fields in your dataset, you will also be able to determine whether you need an algorithm capable of working with categorical data.

2. **Categorize the data problem**: As per the following diagram, in this step, you should analyze your input data to determine if it contains a target feature (a feature whose values you want to be modeled and predicted) or not. Datasets with a target feature are also known as labeled data and are solved using supervised learning (**A**) algorithms. On the other hand, datasets without a target feature are known as unlabeled data and are solved using unsupervised learning algorithms (**B**).

Moreover, the output data (the form of output that you expect from the model) also plays a key role in determining the algorithms to be used. If the output from the model needs to be a continuous number, the task to be solved is a regression problem (**C**). On the other hand, if the output is a discrete value (a set of categories, for instance), the task at hand is a classification problem (**D**). Finally, if the output is a subgroup of observations, the process to be performed is a clustering task (**E**):

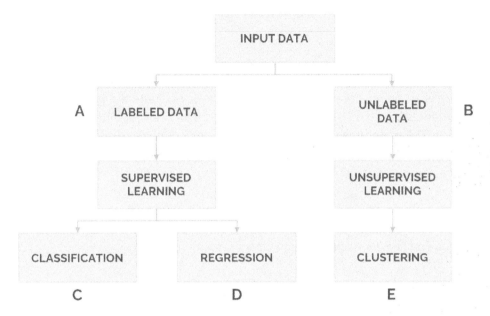

Figure 1.1: Demonstrating the division of tasks

This division of tasks will be explored in more detail in the *Supervised and Unsupervised Learning* section of this chapter.

3. **Choose a set of algorithms**: Once the preceding steps have been performed, it is possible to filter out the algorithms that perform well over the input data and that are able to arrive at the desired outcome. Depending on your resources and time limitations, you should choose from this list of apt algorithms the ones that you want to test out over your data problem, considering that it is always a good practice to try more than one algorithm.

These steps will be explained in more detail in the next chapter using a real-life data problem as an example.

SCIKIT-LEARN

Created in 2007 by David Cournapeau as part of a Google Summer of Code project, scikit-learn is an open source Python library made to facilitate the process of building models based on built-in ML and statistical algorithms, without the need for hardcoding. The main reasons for its popular use are its complete documentation, its easy-to-use API, and the many collaborators who work every day to improve the library.

> **NOTE**
>
> You can find the documentation for scikit-learn at http://scikit-learn.org.

Scikit-learn is mainly used to model data, and not as much to manipulate or summarize data. It offers its users an easy-to-use, uniform API to apply different models with little learning effort, and no real knowledge of the math behind it is required.

> **NOTE**
>
> Some of the math topics that you need to know about to understand the models are linear algebra, probability theory, and multivariate calculus. For more information on these models, visit https://towardsdatascience.com/the-mathematics-of-machine-learning-894f046c568.

The models that are available in the scikit-learn library fall into two categories, that is, supervised and unsupervised, both of which will be explained in depth later in this chapter. This form of category classification will help to determine which model to use for a particular dataset to get the most information out of it.

Besides its main use for predicting future behavior in supervised learning problems and clustering data in unsupervised learning problems, scikit-learn is also used for the following reasons:

- To carry out cross-validation and performance metrics analysis to understand the results that have been obtained from the model, and thereby improve its performance

- To obtain sample datasets to test algorithms on them

- To perform feature extraction to extract features from images or text data

Although scikit-learn is considered the preferred Python library for beginners in the world of ML, there are several large companies around the world that use it because it allows them to improve their products or services by applying the models to already existing developments. It also permits them to quickly implement tests on new ideas.

Some of the leading companies that are using scikit-learn are as follows:

- Spotify: One of the most popular music streaming applications, Spotify makes use of scikit-learn mainly due to the wide variety of algorithms that the framework offers, as well as how easy it is to implement the new models into their current developments. Scikit-learn has been used as part of its music recommendation model.

- Booking.com: From developing recommendation systems to preventing fraudulent activities, among many other solutions, this travel metasearch engine has been able to use scikit-learn to explore a large number of algorithms that allow the creation of state-of-the-art models.

- Evernote: This note-taking and management app uses scikit-learn to tackle several of the steps required to train a classification model, from data exploration to model evaluation.

- Change.org: Thanks to the framework's ease of use and variety of algorithms, this non-profit organization has been able to create email marketing campaigns that reach millions of readers around the world.

> **NOTE**
>
> You can visit http://scikit-learn.org/stable/testimonials/testimonials.html to discover other companies that are using scikit-learn and see what they are using it for.

In conclusion, scikit-learn is an open source Python library that uses an API to apply most ML tasks (both supervised and unsupervised) to data problems. Its main use is for modeling data so that predictions can be made about unseen observations; nevertheless, it should not be limited to that as the library also allows users to predict outcomes based on the model being trained, as well as to analyze the performance of the model, among other features.

ADVANTAGES OF SCIKIT-LEARN

The following is a list of the main advantages of using scikit-learn for ML purposes:

- **Ease of use**: Scikit-learn is characterized by a clean API, with a small learning curve in comparison to other libraries, such as TensorFlow or Keras. The API is popular for its uniformity and straightforward approach. Users of scikit-learn do not necessarily need to understand the math behind the models.

- **Uniformity**: Its uniform API makes it very easy to switch from model to model as the basic syntax that's required for one model is the same for others.

- **Documentation/tutorials**: The library is completely backed up by documentation, which is effortlessly accessible and easy to understand. Additionally, it also offers step-by-step tutorials that cover all of the topics required to develop any ML project.

- **Reliability and collaborations**: As an open source library, scikit-learn benefits from the input of multiple collaborators who work each day to improve its performance. This participation from many experts from different contexts helps to develop not only a more complete library but also a more reliable one.

- **Coverage**: As you scan the list of components that the library has, you will discover that it covers most ML tasks, ranging from supervised models such as performing a regression task to unsupervised models such as the ones used to cluster data into subgroups. Moreover, due to its many collaborators, new models tend to be added in relatively short amounts of time.

DISADVANTAGES OF SCIKIT-LEARN

The following is a list of the main disadvantages of using scikit-learn for ML purposes:

- **Inflexibility**: Due to its ease of use, the library tends to be inflexible. This means that users do not have much liberty in parameter tuning or model architecture, such as with the Gradient Boost algorithm and neural networks. This becomes an issue as beginners move to more complex projects.

- **Not good for deep learning**: The performance of the library falls short when tackling complex ML projects. This is especially true for deep learning, as scikit-learn does not support deep neural networks with the necessary architecture or power.

> **NOTE**
>
> Deep learning is a part of ML and is based on the concept of artificial neural networks. It uses a sequence of layers to extract valuable information (features) from the input data. In subsequent sections of this book, you will learn about neural networks, which is the starting point of being able to develop deep learning solutions.

In general terms, scikit-learn is an excellent beginner's library as it requires little effort to learn its use and has many complementary materials thought to facilitate its application. Due to the contributions of several collaborators, the library stays up to date and is applicable to most current data problems.

On the other hand, it is a simple library that's not fit for more complex data problems such as deep learning. Likewise, it is not recommended for users who wish to take their abilities to a higher level by playing with the different parameters that are available in each model.

OTHER FRAMEWORKS

Other popular ML frameworks are as follows:

- TensorFlow: Google's open source framework for ML, which to this day is still the most popular among data scientists. It is typically integrated with Python and is very good for developing deep learning solutions. Due to its popularity, the information that's available on the internet about the framework makes it very easy to develop different solutions, not to mention that it is backed by Google.

- PyTorch: This was primarily developed by Facebook's AI Research lab as an open source deep learning framework. Although it is a fairly new framework (released in 2017), it has grown in popularity due to its ease of use and Pythonic nature. It allows easy code debugging thanks to the use of dynamic graph computations.

- Keras: This is an open source deep learning framework that's typically good for those who are just starting out. Due to its simplicity, it is less flexible but ideal for prototyping simple concepts. Similar to scikit-learn, it has its own easy-to-use API.

DATA REPRESENTATION

The main objective of ML is to build models by interpreting data. To do so, it is highly important to feed the data in a way that is readable by the computer. To feed data into a scikit-learn model, it must be represented as a table or matrix of the required dimensions, which we will discuss in the following section.

TABLES OF DATA

Most tables that are fed into ML problems are two-dimensional, meaning that they contain rows and columns. Conventionally, each row represents an observation (an instance), whereas each column represents a characteristic (feature) of each observation.

The following table is a fragment of a sample dataset of scikit-learn. The purpose of the dataset is to differentiate from among three types of iris plants based on their characteristics. Hence, in the following table, each row embodies a plant and each column denotes the value of that feature for every plant:

Columns: Features ↓

	sepal_length	sepal_width	petal_length	petal_width	species
0	5.1	3.5	1.4	0.2	setosa
1	4.9	3	1.4	0.2	setosa
2	4.7	3.2	1.3	0.2	setosa
3	4.6	3.1	1.5	0.2	setosa
4	5	3.6	1.4	0.2	setosa
5	5.4	3.9	1.7	0.4	setosa
6	4.6	3.4	1.4	0.3	setosa
7	5	3.4	1.5	0.2	setosa
8	4.4	2.9	1.4	0.2	setosa
9	4.9	3.1	1.5	0.1	setosa

Rows: Observations/Instances

Figure 1.2: A table showing the first 10 instances of the iris dataset

From the preceding explanation, by reviewing the first row of the preceding table, it is possible to determine that the observation corresponds to that of a plant with a sepal length of 5.1, a sepal width of 3.5, a petal length of 1.4, and a petal width of 0.2. The plant belongs to the **setosa** species.

NOTE

When feeding images to a model, the tables become three-dimensional, where the rows and columns represent the dimensions of the image in pixels, while the depth represents its color scheme. If you are interested, feel free to find out more about *convolutional neural networks*.

Data in tables are also known as structured data. Unstructured data, on the other hand, refers to everything else that cannot be stored in a table-like database (that is, in rows and columns). This includes images, audio, videos, and text (such as emails or reviews). To be able to feed unstructured data into an ML algorithm, the first step should be to transform it into a format that the algorithm can understand (tables of data). For instance, images are converted into matrices of pixels, and text is encoded into numeric values.

FEATURES AND TARGET MATRICES

For many data problems, one of the features of your dataset will be used as a **label**. This means that out of all the other features, this one is the target that the model should generalize the data to. For example, in the preceding table, we might choose the species as the target feature, so we would like the model to find patterns based on the other features to determine whether a plant belongs to the **setosa** species. Therefore, it is important to learn how to separate the target matrix from the features matrix.

Features Matrix: The features matrix comprises data from each instance for all features, except the target. It can be either created using a NumPy array or a Pandas DataFrame, and its dimensions are `[n_i, n_f]`, where `n_i` denotes the number of instances (such as the universe of persons in the dataset) and `n_f` denotes the number of features (such as the demographics of each person). Generally, the features matrix is stored in a variable named **X**.

> ### NOTE
>
> Pandas is an open source library built for Python. It was created to tackle different tasks related to data manipulation and analysis. Likewise, NumPy an open source Python library and is used to manipulate large multi-dimensional arrays. It was also created with a large set of mathematical functions to operate over such arrays.

Target Matrix: Different to the features matrix, the target matrix is usually one-dimensional since it only carries one feature for all instances, meaning that its length is `n_i` (the number of instances). Nevertheless, there are some occasions where multiple targets are required, so the dimensions of the matrix become `[n_i, n_t]`, where `n_t` is the number of targets to consider.

Similar to the features matrix, the target matrix is usually created as a NumPy array or a Pandas series. The values of the target array may be discrete or continuous. Generally, the target matrix is stored in a variable named **Y**.

EXERCISE 1.01: LOADING A SAMPLE DATASET AND CREATING THE FEATURES AND TARGET MATRICES

> **NOTE**
>
> All of the exercises and activities in this book will be primarily developed in Jupyter Notebooks. It is recommended to keep a separate Notebook for different assignments, unless advised otherwise. Also, to load a sample dataset, the **seaborn** library will be used, as it displays the data as a table. Other ways to load data will be explained in later sections.

In this exercise, we will be loading the **tips** dataset from the **seaborn** library and creating features and target matrices using it. Follow these steps to complete this exercise:

> **NOTE**
>
> For the exercises and activities within this chapter, ensure that you have Python 3.7, Seaborn 0.9, Jupyter 6.0, Matplotlib 3.1, NumPy 1.18, and Pandas 0.25 installed on your system.

1. Open a Jupyter Notebook to complete this exercise. In the Command Prompt or Terminal, navigate to the desired path and use the following command:

```
jupyter notebook
```

2. Load the **tips** dataset using the **seaborn** library. To do so, you need to import the **seaborn** library and then use the **load_dataset()** function, as shown in the following code:

```
import seaborn as sns
tips = sns.load_dataset('tips')
```

As we can see from the preceding code, after importing the library, a nickname is given to facilitate its use with the script.

The **load_dataset()** function loads datasets from an online repository. The data from the dataset is stored in a variable named **tips**.

3. Create a variable, **X**, to store the features. Use the **drop()** function to include all of the features but the target, which in this case is named **tip**. Then, print out the top 10 instances of the variable:

```
X = tips.drop('tip', axis=1)
X.head(10)
```

> **NOTE**
>
> The **axis** parameter in the preceding snippet denotes whether you want to drop the label from rows (**axis = 0**) or columns (**axis = 1**).

The printed output should look as follows:

	total_bill	sex	smoker	day	time	size
0	16.99	Female	No	Sun	Dinner	2
1	10.34	Male	No	Sun	Dinner	3
2	21.01	Male	No	Sun	Dinner	3
3	23.68	Male	No	Sun	Dinner	2
4	24.59	Female	No	Sun	Dinner	4
5	25.29	Male	No	Sun	Dinner	4
6	8.77	Male	No	Sun	Dinner	2
7	26.88	Male	No	Sun	Dinner	4
8	15.04	Male	No	Sun	Dinner	2
9	14.78	Male	No	Sun	Dinner	2

Figure 1.3: A table showing the first 10 instances of the features matrix

4. Print the shape of your new variable using the **X.shape** command:

    ```
    X.shape
    ```

    The output is as follows:

    ```
    (244, 6)
    ```

    The first value indicates the number of instances in the dataset (**244**), while the second value represents the number of features (**6**).

5. Create a variable, **Y**, that will store the target values. There is no need to use a function for this. Use indexing to grab only the desired column. Indexing allows you to access a section of a larger element. In this case, we want to grab the column named **tip**. Then, we need to print out the top 10 values of the variable:

    ```
    Y = tips['tip']
    Y.head(10)
    ```

    The printed output should look as follows:

    ```
    0      1.01
    1      1.66
    2      3.50
    3      3.31
    4      3.61
    5      4.71
    6      2.00
    7      3.12
    8      1.96
    9      3.23
    Name: tip, dtype: float64
    ```

    Figure 1.4: A screenshot showing the first 10 instances of the target matrix

6. Print the shape of your new variable using the **Y.shape** command:

    ```
    Y.shape
    ```

    The output is as follows:

    ```
    (244,)
    ```

The shape should be one-dimensional with a length equal to the number of instances (**244**).

> **NOTE**
>
> To access the source code for this specific section, please refer to https://packt.live/2Y5dgZH.
>
> You can also run this example online at https://packt.live/3d0Hsco. You must execute the entire Notebook in order to get the desired result.

With that, you have successfully created the features and target matrices of a dataset.

Generally, the preferred way to represent data is by using two-dimensional tables, where the rows represent the number of observations, also known as instances, and the columns represent the characteristics of those instances, commonly known as features.

For data problems that require target labels, the data table needs to be partitioned into a features matrix and a target matrix. The features matrix will contain the values of all features but the target, for each instance, making it a two-dimensional matrix. On the other hand, the target matrix will only contain the value of the target feature for all entries, making it a one-dimensional matrix.

ACTIVITY 1.01: SELECTING A TARGET FEATURE AND CREATING A TARGET MATRIX

You want to analyze the Titanic dataset to see the survival rate of the passengers on different decks and see if you can prove a hypothesis stating that passengers on the lower decks were less likely to survive. In this activity, we will attempt to load a dataset and create the features and target matrices by choosing the appropriate target feature for the objective at hand.

> **NOTE**
>
> To choose the target feature, remember that the target should be the outcome that we want to interpret the data for. For instance, if we want to know what features play a role in determining a plant's species, the species should be the target value.

Follow these steps to complete this activity:

1. Load the **titanic** dataset using the **seaborn** library. The first couple of rows should look like this:

	survived	pclass	sex	age	sibsp	parch	fare	embarked	class	who	adult_male	deck	embark_town	alive	alone
0	0	3	male	22.0	1	0	7.2500	S	Third	man	True	NaN	Southampton	no	False
1	1	1	female	38.0	1	0	71.2833	C	First	woman	False	C	Cherbourg	yes	False
2	1	3	female	26.0	0	0	7.9250	S	Third	woman	False	NaN	Southampton	yes	True
3	1	1	female	35.0	1	0	53.1000	S	First	woman	False	C	Southampton	yes	False
4	0	3	male	35.0	0	0	8.0500	S	Third	man	True	NaN	Southampton	no	True
5	0	3	male	NaN	0	0	8.4583	Q	Third	man	True	NaN	Queenstown	no	True
6	0	1	male	54.0	0	0	51.8625	S	First	man	True	E	Southampton	no	True
7	0	3	male	2.0	3	1	21.0750	S	Third	child	False	NaN	Southampton	no	False
8	1	3	female	27.0	0	2	11.1333	S	Third	woman	False	NaN	Southampton	yes	False
9	1	2	female	14.0	1	0	30.0708	C	Second	child	False	NaN	Cherbourg	yes	False

Figure 1.5: A table showing the first 10 instances of the Titanic dataset

2. Select your preferred target feature for the goal of this activity.

3. Create both the features matrix and the target matrix. Make sure that you store the data from the features matrix in a variable, **X**, and the data from the target matrix in another variable, **Y**.

4. Print out the shape of each of the matrices, which should match the following values:

```
Features matrix: (891, 14)
Target matrix: (891,)
```

> **NOTE**
>
> The solution for this activity can be found on page 210.

DATA PREPROCESSING

Data preprocessing is a very critical step for developing ML solutions as it helps make sure that the model is not trained on biased data. It has the capability to improve a model's performance, and it is often the reason why the same algorithm for the same data problem works better for a programmer that has done an outstanding job preprocessing the dataset.

For the computer to be able to understand the data proficiently, it is necessary to not only feed the data in a standardized way but also make sure that the data does not contain outliers or noisy data, or even missing entries. This is important because failing to do so might result in the algorithm making assumptions that are not true to the data. This will cause the model to train at a slower pace and to be less accurate due to misleading interpretations of data.

Moreover, data preprocessing does not end there. Models do not work the same way, and each one makes different assumptions. This means that we need to preprocess the data in terms of the model that is going to be used. For example, some models accept only numerical data, whereas others work with nominal and numerical data.

To achieve better results during data preprocessing, a good practice is to transform (preprocess) the data in different ways and then test the different transformations in different models. That way, you will be able to select the right transformation for the right model. It is worth mentioning that data preprocessing is likely to help any data problem and any ML algorithm, considering that just by standardizing the dataset, a better training speed is achieved.

MESSY DATA

Data that is missing information or that contains outliers or noise is considered to be **messy data**. Failing to perform any preprocessing to transform the data can lead to poorly created models of the data, due to the introduction of bias and information loss. Some of the issues with data that should be avoided will be explained here.

MISSING VALUES

Both the features and instances of a dataset can have missing values. Features where a few instances have values, as well as instances where there are no values for any feature, are considered **missing data**:

ID	Feature 1	Feature 2	Feature 3	Feature 4	Feature 5	Feature 6	Feature 7	Feature 8
Instance 1		1	3	5	6	8	1	
Instance 2	4	5	2	6	7	2	1	3
Instance 3	2		7	5	9	8	1	
Instance 4	1	2	7	5	2	1	6	
Instance 5	5	8	4	4	6	7	8	5
Instance 6	4	5	9	1	3	4	6	
Instance 7	7	6	5		4	8	6	
Instance 8								
Instance 9	8	2	3	1	2	4	5	3
Instance 10	4	5	9	6	4	9	7	

INSTANCE MISSING VALUES   FEATURE MISSING VALUES

Figure 1.6: Example of missing values

The preceding image displays an instance (Instance 8) with no values for any of the features, which makes it useless, and a feature (Feature 8) with seven missing values out of the 10 instances, which means that the feature cannot be used to find patterns among the instances, considering that most of them don't have a value for the feature.

Conventionally, a feature missing more than 5 to 10% of its values is considered to be missing data (also known as a feature with high absence rate), and so it needs to be dealt with. On the other hand, all instances that have missing values for all features should be eliminated as they do not provide any information to the model and, on the contrary, may end up introducing bias.

When dealing with a feature with a high absence rate, it is recommended to either eliminate it or fill it with values. The most popular ways to replace the missing values are as follows:

- **Mean imputation**: Replacing missing values with the mean or median of the features' available values

- **Regression imputation**: Replacing missing values with the predicted values that have been obtained from a regression function

> **NOTE**
>
> A regression function refers to the statistical model that's used to estimate a relationship between a dependent variable and one or more independent variables. A regression function can be linear, logistic, polynomial, and so on.

While mean imputation is a simpler approach to implement, it may introduce bias as it evens out all the instances. On the other hand, even though the regression approach matches the data to its predicted value, it may end up overfitting the model (that is, creating models that learn the training data too well and are not fit to deal with new unseen data) as all the values that are introduced follow a function.

Lastly, when the missing values are found in a text feature such as gender, the best course of action would be to either eliminate them or replace them with a class labeled as *uncategorized* or something similar. This is mainly because it is not possible to apply either mean or regression imputation to text.

Labeling missing values with a new category (*uncategorized*) is mostly done when eliminating them would remove an important part of the dataset, and hence would not be an appropriate course of action. In this case, even though the new label may have an effect on the model, depending on the rationale that's used to label the missing values, leaving them empty would be an even worse alternative as it would cause the model to make assumptions on its own.

> **NOTE**
>
> To learn more about how to detect and handle missing values, visit the following page: https://towardsdatascience.com/how-to-handle-missing-data-8646b18db0d4.

OUTLIERS

Outliers are values that are far from the mean. This means that if the values from a feature follow a Gaussian distribution, the outliers are located at the tails.

> **NOTE**
>
> A Gaussian distribution (also known as a normal distribution) has a bell-shaped curve, given that there is an equal number of values above and below the mean.

Outliers can be global or local. The former group represents those values that are far from the entire set of values for a feature. For example, when analyzing data from all members of a neighborhood, a global outlier would be a person who is 180 years old (as shown in the following diagram (**A**)). The latter, on the other hand, represents values that are far from a subgroup of values of that feature. For the same example that we saw previously, a local outlier would be a college student who is 70 years old (**B**), which would normally differ from other college students in that neighborhood:

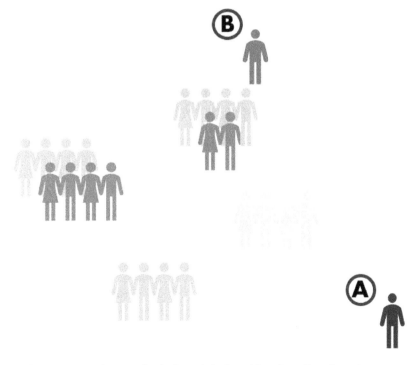

Figure 1.7: An image depicting global and local outliers in a dataset

Considering both examples that have been given, outliers do not evaluate whether the value is possible. While a person aged 180 years is not plausible, a 70-year-old college student might be a possibility, yet both are categorized as outliers as they can both affect the performance of the model.

A straightforward approach to detect outliers consists of visualizing the data to determine whether it follows a Gaussian distribution, and if it does, classifying those values that fall between three to six standard deviations away from the mean as outliers. Nevertheless, there is not an exact rule to determine an outlier, and the decision to select the number of standard deviations is subjective and will vary from problem to problem.

For example, if the dataset is reduced by 40% by setting three standard deviations as the parameter to rule out values, it would be appropriate to change the number of standard deviations to four.

On the other hand, when dealing with text features, detecting outliers becomes even trickier as there are no standard deviations to use. In this case, counting the occurrences of each class value would help to determine whether a certain class is indispensable or not. For instance, in clothing sizes, having a size XXS that represents less than 5% of the entire dataset might not be necessary.

Once the outliers have been detected, there are three common ways to handle them:

- **Delete the outlier**: For outliers that are true values, it is best to completely delete them to avoid skewing the analysis. This may also be a good idea for outliers that are mistakes, that is, if the number of outliers is too large to perform further analysis to assign a new value.

- **Define a top**: Defining a top may also be useful for true values. For instance, if you realize that all values above a certain threshold behave the same way, you can consider topping that value with a threshold.

- **Assign a new value**: If the outlier is clearly a mistake, you can assign a new value using one of the techniques that we discussed for missing values (mean or regression imputation).

The decision to use each of the preceding approaches depends on the outlier type and number. Most of the time, if the number of outliers represents a small proportion of the total size of the dataset, there is no point in treating the outlier in any way other than deleting it.

> **NOTE**
>
> Noisy data corresponds to values that are not correct or possible. This includes numerical (outliers that are mistakes) and nominal values (for example, a person's gender misspelled as "fimale"). Like outliers, noisy data can be treated by deleting the values completely or by assigning them a new value.

EXERCISE 1.02: DEALING WITH MESSY DATA

In this exercise, we will be using the **tips** dataset from seaborn as an example to demonstrate how to deal with messy data. Follow these steps to complete this exercise:

1. Open a Jupyter Notebook to implement this exercise.

2. Import all the required elements. Next, load the **tips** dataset and store it in a variable called **tips**. Use the following code:

```
import seaborn as sns
import numpy as np
import matplotlib.pyplot as plt
tips = sns.load_dataset('tips')
```

3. Next, create a variable called **size** to store the values of that feature from the dataset. As this dataset does not contain any missing data, we will convert the top 16 values of the **size** variable into missing values. Print out the top 20 values of the **age** variable:

```
size = tips["size"]
size.loc[:15] = np.nan
size.head(20)
```

> **NOTE**
>
> A warning may appear at this point, saying *A value is trying to be set on a copy of a slice from a DataFrame*. This occurs because `size` is a slice of the **tips** dataset, and by making a change in the slice, the dataset is also changed. This is okay as the purpose of this exercise is to modify the dataset by modifying the different features that it contains.

The preceding code snippet creates the size variable as a slice of the dataset, then coverts the top 16 values of the variable into Not a Number (**NaN**), which is the representation of a missing value. Finally, it prints the top 20 values of the variable.

The output will appear as follows:

```
0      NaN
1      NaN
2      NaN
3      NaN
4      NaN
5      NaN
6      NaN
7      NaN
8      NaN
9      NaN
10     NaN
11     NaN
12     NaN
13     NaN
14     NaN
15     NaN
16     3.0
17     3.0
18     3.0
19     3.0
Name: size, dtype: float64
```

Figure 1.8: A screenshot showing the first 20 instances of the age variable

As you can see, the feature contains the **NaN** values that we introduced.

4. Check the shape of the **size** variable:

```
size.shape
```

The output is as follows:

```
(244,)
```

5. Now, count the number of **NaN** values to determine how to handle them. Use the **isnull()** function to find the **NaN** values, and use the **sum()** function to sum them all:

```
size.isnull().sum()
```

The output is as follows:

```
16
```

The participation of the **NaN** values in the total size of the variable is 6.55%, which can be calculated by dividing the number of missing values by the length of the feature (16/244). Although this is not high enough to consider removing the entire feature, there is a need to handle the missing values.

6. Let's choose the mean imputation methodology to replace the missing values. To do so, compute the mean of the available values, as follows:

```
mean = size.mean()
mean = round(mean)
print(mean)
```

The mean comes out as **3**.

> **NOTE**
>
> The mean value (**2.55**) was rounded to its nearest integer since the **size** feature is a measure of the number of persons attending a restaurant.

7. Replace all missing values with the mean. Use the **fillna()** function, which takes every missing value and replaces it with the value that is defined inside the parenthesis. To check that the values have been replaced, print the first 10 values again:

```
size.fillna(mean, inplace=True)
size.head(20)
```

> **NOTE**
>
> When **inplace** is set to **True**, the original DataFrame is modified. Failing to set the parameter to **True** will leave the original dataset unmodified. According to this, by setting **inplace** to **True**, it is possible to replace the **NaN** values for the mean.

The printed output is as follows:

```
0      3.0
1      3.0
2      3.0
3      3.0
4      3.0
5      3.0
6      3.0
7      3.0
8      3.0
9      3.0
10     3.0
11     3.0
12     3.0
13     3.0
14     3.0
15     3.0
16     3.0
17     3.0
18     3.0
19     3.0
Name: size, dtype: float64
```

Figure 1.9: A screenshot depicting the first 20 instances of the age variable

As shown in the preceding screenshot, the value of the top instances has changed from **NaN** to **3**, which is the mean that was calculated previously.

8. Use Matplotlib to graph a histogram of the **age** variable. Use Matplotlib's **hist()** function, as per the following code:

```
plt.hist(size)
plt.show()
```

The histogram should look as follows. As we can see, its distribution is Gaussian-like:

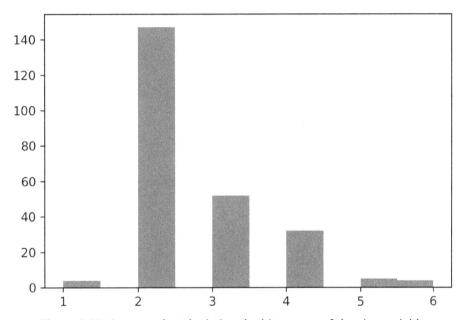

Figure 1.10: A screenshot depicting the histogram of the size variable

9. Discover the outliers in the data. Let's use three standard deviations as the measure to calculate the minimum and maximum values.

As we discussed previously, the min value is determined by calculating the mean of all of the values and subtracting three standard deviations from it. Use the following code to set the min value and store it in a variable named **min_val**:

```
min_val = size.mean() - (3 * size.std())
print(min_val)
```

The min value is around **-0.1974**. According to the min value, there are no outliers at the left tail of the Gaussian distribution. This makes sense, given that the distribution is tilted slightly to the left.

Opposite to the min value, for the max value, the standard deviations are added to the mean to calculate the higher threshold. Calculate the max value, as shown in the following code, and store it in a variable named **max_val**:

```
max_val = size.mean() + (3 * size.std())
print(max_val)
```

The max value, which comes to around **5.3695**, determines that instances with a size above 5.36 represent outliers. As you can see in the preceding diagram, this also makes sense as those instances are far away from the bell of the Gaussian distribution.

10. Count the number of instances that are above the maximum value to decide how to handle them, as per the instructions given here.

    Using indexing, obtain the values in **size** that are above the max threshold and store them in a variable called **outliers**. Then, count the outliers using **count()**:

    ```
    outliers = size[size > max_val]
    outliers.count()
    ```

    The output shows that there are **4** outliers.

11. Print out the outliers and check that the correct values were stored, as follows:

    ```
    print(outliers)
    ```

    The output is as follows:

    ```
    125      6.0
    141      6.0
    143      6.0
    156      6.0
    Name: size, dtype: float64
    ```

    Figure 1.11: Printing the outliers

As the number of outliers is small, and they correspond to true outliers, they can be deleted.

> **NOTE**
>
> For this exercise, we will be deleting the instances from the `size` variable to understand the complete procedure of dealing with outliers. However, later, the deletion of outliers will be handled while considering all of the features so that we can delete the entire instance, not just the size values.

12. Redefine the values stored in `size` by using indexing to include only values below the max threshold. Then, print the shape of `size`:

```
age = size[size <= max_val]
age.shape
```

The output is as follows:

```
(240,)
```

As you can see, the shape of `size` (calculated in *Step 4*) has been reduced by four, which was the number of outliers.

> **NOTE**
>
> To access the source code for this specific section, please refer to https://packt.live/30EgkOo.
>
> You can also run this example online at https://packt.live/3d321ow.
> You must execute the entire Notebook in order to get the desired result.

You have successfully cleaned a Pandas series. This process serves as a guide for cleaning a dataset later on.

To summarize, we have discussed the importance of preprocessing data, as failing to do so may introduce bias in the model, which affects the training time of the model and its performance. Some of the main forms of messy data are missing values, outliers, and noise.

Missing values, as their name suggests, are those values that are left empty or null. When dealing with many missing values, it is important to handle them by deleting them or by assigning new values. Two ways to assign new values were also discussed: mean imputation and regression imputation.

Outliers are values that fall far from the mean of all the values of a feature. One way to detect outliers is by selecting all the values that fall outside the mean plus/minus three/six standard deviations. Outliers may be mistakes (values that are not possible) or true values, and they should be handled differently. While true outliers may be deleted or topped, mistakes should be replaced with other values when possible.

Finally, noisy data corresponds to values that are, regardless of their proximity to the mean, mistakes or typos in the data. They can be of numeric, ordinal, or nominal types.

> **NOTE**
>
> Please remember that numeric data is always represented by numbers that can be measured, nominal data refers to text data that does not follow a rank, and ordinal data refers to text data that follows a rank or order.

DEALING WITH CATEGORICAL FEATURES

Categorical features are features that comprise discrete values typically belonging to a finite set of categories. Categorical data can be nominal or ordinal. Nominal refers to categories that do not follow a specific order, such as music genre or city names, whereas ordinal refers to categories with a sense of order, such as clothing sizes or level of education.

FEATURE ENGINEERING

Even though improvements in many ML algorithms have enabled the algorithms to understand categorical data types such as text, the process of transforming them into numeric values facilitates the training process of the model, which results in faster running times and better performance. This is mainly due to the elimination of semantics available in each category, as well as the fact that the conversion into numeric values allows you to scale all of the features of the dataset equally, as will be explained in subsequent sections of this chapter.

How does it work? Feature engineering generates a label encoding that assigns a numeric value to each category; this value will then replace the category in the dataset. For example, a variable called **genre** with the classes **pop**, **rock**, and **country** can be converted as follows:

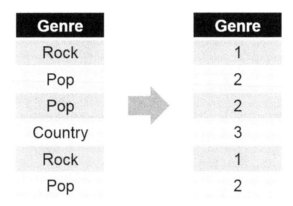

Figure 1.12: An image illustrating how feature engineering works

EXERCISE 1.03: APPLYING FEATURE ENGINEERING TO TEXT DATA

In this exercise, we will be converting the text features of the **tips** dataset into numerical data.

> **NOTE**
>
> Use the same Jupyter Notebook that you created for the previous exercise.

Follow these steps to complete this exercise:

1. Import scikit-learn's **LabelEncoder()** class, as well as the **pandas** library, as follows:

```
from sklearn.preprocessing import LabelEncoder
import pandas as pd
```

2. Convert each of the text features into numeric values using the class that was imported previously (**LabelEncoder**):

```
enc = LabelEncoder()
tips["sex"] = enc.fit_transform(tips['sex'].astype('str'))
tips["smoker"] = enc.fit_transform(tips['smoker'].astype('str'))
tips["day"] = enc.fit_transform(tips['day'].astype('str'))
tips["time"] = enc.fit_transform(tips['time'].astype('str'))
```

As per the preceding code snippet, the first step is to instantiate the **LabelEncoder** class by typing in the first line of code. Second, for each of the categorical features, we use the built-in **fit_transform()** method from the class, which will assign a numeric value to each category and output the result.

3. Print out the top values of the **tips** dataset:

```
tips.head()
```

The output is as follows:

	total_bill	tip	sex	smoker	day	time	size
0	16.99	1.01	0	0	2	0	3.0
1	10.34	1.66	1	0	2	0	3.0
2	21.01	3.50	1	0	2	0	3.0
3	23.68	3.31	1	0	2	0	3.0
4	24.59	3.61	0	0	2	0	3.0

Figure 1.13: A screenshot depicting the first five instances of the tips dataset

As you can see, the text categories of the categorical features have been converted into numeric values.

> **NOTE**
>
> To access the source code for this specific section, please refer to https://packt.live/30GWJgb.
>
> You can also run this example online at https://packt.live/3e2oaVu. You must execute the entire Notebook in order to get the desired result.

You have successfully converted text data into numeric values.

While improvements in ML have made dealing with text features easier for some algorithms, it is best to convert them into numeric values. This is mainly important as it eliminates the complexity of dealing with semantics, not to mention that it gives us the flexibility to change from model to model, without any limitations.

Text data conversion is done via feature engineering, where every text category is assigned a numeric value that replaces it. Furthermore, even though this can be done manually, there are powerful built-in classes and methods that facilitate this process. One example of this is the use of scikit-learn's **LabelEncoder** class.

RESCALING DATA

Rescaling data is important because even though the data may be fed to a model using different scales for each feature, the lack of homogeneity can cause the algorithm to lose its ability to discover patterns from the data due to the assumptions it has to make to understand it, thereby slowing down the training process and negatively affecting the model's performance.

Data rescaling helps the model run faster, without any burden or responsibility to learn from the invariance present in the dataset. Moreover, a model trained over equally scaled data assigns the same weights (level of importance) to all parameters, which allows the algorithm to generalize to all features and not just to those with higher values, irrespective of their meaning.

An example of a dataset with different scales is one that contains different features, one measured in kilograms, another measuring temperature, and another counting the number of children. Even though the values of each attribute are true, the scale of each one of them highly differs from that of the other. For example, while the values in kilograms can go higher than 100, the children count will typically not go higher than 10.

Two of the most popular ways to rescale data are **data normalization** and **data standardization**. There is no rule on selecting the methodology to transform data to scale it, as all datasets behave differently. The best practice is to transform the data using two or three rescaling methodologies and test the algorithms in each one of them in order to choose the one that best fits the data based on its performance.

Rescaling methodologies are to be used individually. When testing different rescaling methodologies, the transformation of data should be done independently. Each transformation can be tested over a model, and the best suited one should be chosen for further steps.

Normalization: Data normalization in ML consists of rescaling the values of all features so that they lie in a range between 0 and 1 and have a maximum length of one. This serves the purpose of equating attributes of different scales.

The following equation allows you to normalize the values of a feature:

$$z_i = \frac{x_i - \min(x)}{\max(x) - \min(x)}$$

Figure 1.14: The normalization equation

Here, z_i corresponds to the ith normalized value and x represents all values.

Standardization: This is a rescaling technique that transforms the data into a Gaussian distribution with a mean equal to 0 and a standard deviation equal to 1.

One simple way of standardizing a feature is shown in the following equation:

$$z_i = \frac{x_i - mean(x)}{std(x)}$$

Figure 1.15: The standardization equation

Here, z_i corresponds to the ith standardized value and x represents all values.

EXERCISE 1.04: NORMALIZING AND STANDARDIZING DATA

This exercise covers the normalization and standardization of data, using the **tips** dataset as an example.

> **NOTE**
>
> Use the same Jupyter Notebook that you created for the previous exercise.

Follow these steps to complete this exercise:

1. Using the **tips** variable, which contains the entire dataset, normalize the data using the normalization formula and store it in a new variable called **tips_normalized**. Print out the top 10 values:

```
tips_normalized = (tips - tips.min())/(tips.max()-tips.min())
tips_normalized.head(10)
```

The output is as follows:

	total_bill	tip	sex	smoker	day	time	size
0	0.291579	0.001111	0.0	0.0	0.666667	0.0	0.4
1	0.152283	0.073333	1.0	0.0	0.666667	0.0	0.4
2	0.375786	0.277778	1.0	0.0	0.666667	0.0	0.4
3	0.431713	0.256667	1.0	0.0	0.666667	0.0	0.4
4	0.450775	0.290000	0.0	0.0	0.666667	0.0	0.4
5	0.465438	0.412222	1.0	0.0	0.666667	0.0	0.4
6	0.119397	0.111111	1.0	0.0	0.666667	0.0	0.4
7	0.498743	0.235556	1.0	0.0	0.666667	0.0	0.4
8	0.250733	0.106667	1.0	0.0	0.666667	0.0	0.4
9	0.245287	0.247778	1.0	0.0	0.666667	0.0	0.4

Figure 1.16: A screenshot displaying the first 10 instances of the tips_normalized variable

As shown in the preceding screenshot, all of the values have been converted into their equivalents in a range between 0 and 1. By performing normalization for all of the features, the model will be trained on features of the same scale.

2. Again, using the **tips** variable, standardize the data using the formula for standardization and store it in a variable called **tips_standardized**. Print out the top 10 values:

```
tips_standardized = (tips - tips.mean())/tips.std()
tips_standardized.head(10)
```

The output is as follows:

	total_bill	tip	sex	smoker	day	time	size
0	-0.314066	-1.436993	-1.340598	-0.783179	0.278585	-0.620307	0.44613
1	-1.061054	-0.967217	0.742879	-0.783179	0.278585	-0.620307	0.44613
2	0.137497	0.362610	0.742879	-0.783179	0.278585	-0.620307	0.44613
3	0.437416	0.225291	0.742879	-0.783179	0.278585	-0.620307	0.44613
4	0.539635	0.442111	-1.340598	-0.783179	0.278585	-0.620307	0.44613
5	0.618266	1.237116	0.742879	-0.783179	0.278585	-0.620307	0.44613
6	-1.237411	-0.721488	0.742879	-0.783179	0.278585	-0.620307	0.44613
7	0.796869	0.087972	0.742879	-0.783179	0.278585	-0.620307	0.44613
8	-0.533108	-0.750398	0.742879	-0.783179	0.278585	-0.620307	0.44613
9	-0.562313	0.167472	0.742879	-0.783179	0.278585	-0.620307	0.44613

Figure 1.17: A screenshot displaying the first 10 instances of the tips_standardized variable

Compared to normalization, in standardization, the values distribute normally around zero.

> **NOTE**
>
> To access the source code for this specific section, please refer to https://packt.live/30FKsbD.
>
> You can also run this example online at https://packt.live/3e3cW2O.
> You must execute the entire Notebook in order to get the desired result.

You have successfully applied rescaling methods to your data.

In conclusion, we have covered the final step in data preprocessing, which consists of rescaling data. This process was done in a dataset with features of different scales, with the objective of homogenizing the way data is represented to facilitate the comprehension of the data by the model.

Failing to rescale data will cause the model to train at a slower pace and may negatively affect the performance of the model.

Two methodologies for data rescaling were explained in this topic: normalization and standardization. On one hand, normalization transforms the data to a length of one (from 0 to 1). On the other hand, standardization converts the data into a Gaussian distribution with a mean of 0 and a standard deviation of 1.

Given that there is no rule for selecting the appropriate rescaling methodology, the recommended course of action is to transform the data using two or three rescaling methodologies independently, and then train the model with each transformation to evaluate the methodology that behaves the best.

ACTIVITY 1.02: PRE-PROCESSING AN ENTIRE DATASET

You are continuing to work for the safety department at a cruise company. As you did great work selecting the ideal target feature to develop the study, the department has decided to commission you for preprocessing the dataset as well. For this purpose, you need to use all the techniques you learned about previously to preprocess the dataset and get it ready for model training. The following steps serve to guide you in that direction:

1. Import **seaborn** and the **LabelEncoder** class from scikit-learn. Next, load the Titanic dataset and create the features matrix, including the following features: **sex**, **age**, **fare**, **class**, **embark_town**, and **alone**.

   > NOTE
   >
   > For this activity, the features matrix has been created using only six features since some of the other features were redundant for this study. For example, there is no need to keep both **sex** and **gender**.

2. Check for missing values and outliers in all the features of the features matrix (**X**). Choose a methodology to handle them.

3. Convert all text features into their numeric representations.

4. Rescale your data, either by normalizing or standardizing it.

> **NOTE**
>
> The solution for this activity can be found on page 211.

Expected Output: Results may vary, depending on the choices you make. However, you must be left with a dataset with no missing values, outliers, or text features, and with the data rescaled.

SCIKIT-LEARN API

The objective of the scikit-learn API is to provide an efficient and unified syntax to make ML accessible to non-ML experts, as well as to facilitate and popularize its use among several industries.

HOW DOES IT WORK?

Although it has many collaborators, the scikit-learn API was built and has been updated by considering a set of principles that prevent framework code proliferation, where different code performs similar functionalities. On the contrary, it promotes simple conventions and consistency. Due to this, the scikit-learn API is consistent among all models, and once the main functionalities have been learned, it can be used widely.

The scikit-learn API is divided into three complementary interfaces that share a common syntax and logic: the estimator, the predictor, and the transformer. The estimator interface is used for creating models and fitting the data into them; the predictor, as its name suggests, is used to make predictions based on the models that were trained previously; and finally, the transformer is used for converting data.

ESTIMATOR

This is considered to be the core of the entire API, as it is the interface in charge of fitting the models to the input data. It works by instantiating the model to be used and then applies a `fit()` method, which triggers the learning process so that it builds a model based on the data.

The **fit()** method receives the training data as arguments in two separate variables: the features matrix and the target matrix (conventionally called **X_train** and **Y_train**). For unsupervised models, this method only takes in the first argument (**X_train**).

This method creates the model trained to the input data, which can later be used for predicting.

Some models take other arguments besides the training data, which are also called **hyperparameters**. These hyperparameters are initially set to their default values but can be tuned to improve the performance of the model, which will be discussed in later sections.

The following is an example of a model being trained:

```
from sklearn.naive_bayes import GaussianNB
model = GaussianNB()
model.fit(X_train, Y_train)
```

First, it is required that you import the type of algorithm to be used from scikit-learn; for example, a Gaussian Naïve Bayes algorithm (which will be further explored in *Chapter 4, Supervised Learning Algorithms: Predicting Annual Income*) for classification. It is always good practice to import only the algorithm to be used, and not the entire library, as this will ensure that your code runs faster.

> **NOTE**
>
> To find the syntax for importing a different model, use the documentation of scikit-learn. Go to the following link, click the algorithm that you wish to implement, and you will find the instructions there: http://scikit-learn.org/stable/user_guide.html.

The second line of code oversees the instantiation of the model and stores it in a variable. Lastly, the model is fitted to the input data.

In addition to this, the estimator also offers other complementary tasks, as follows:

- Feature extraction, which involves transforming input data into numerical features that can be used for ML purposes.

- Feature selection, which selects the features in your data that contribute to the prediction output of the model.

- Dimensionality reduction, which takes high-dimensional data and converts it into a lower dimension.

PREDICTOR

As explained previously, the predictor takes the model created by the estimator and uses it to perform predictions on unseen data. In general terms, for supervised models, it feeds the model a new set of data, usually called **X_test**, to get a corresponding target or label based on the parameters that were learned while training the model.

Moreover, some unsupervised models can also benefit from the predictor. While this method does not output a specific target value, it can be useful to assign a new instance to a cluster.

Following the preceding example, the implementation of the predictor can be seen as follows:

```
Y_pred = model.predict(X_test)
```

We apply the **predict()** method to the previously trained model and input the new data as an argument to the method.

In addition to predicting, the predictor can also implement methods that are in charge of quantifying the confidence of the prediction (that is, a numeric value representative of the level of performance of the model). These performance measures vary from model to model, but their main objective is to determine how far the prediction is from reality. This is done by taking an **X_test** with its corresponding **Y_test** and comparing it to the predictions made with the same **X_test**.

TRANSFORMER

As we saw previously, data is usually transformed before being fed to a model. Considering this, the API contains a **transform()** method that allows you to perform some preprocessing techniques.

It can be used both as a starting point to transform the input data of the model (**X_train**), as well as further along to modify data that will be fed to the model for predictions. This latter application is crucial to get accurate results as it ensures that the new data follows the same distribution as the data that was used to train the model.

The following is an example of a transformer that normalizes the values of the training data:

```
from sklearn.preprocessing import StandardScaler
scaler = StandardScaler()
scaler.fit(X_train)
X_train = scaler.transform(X_train)
```

The **StandardScaler** class standardizes the data that it receives as arguments. As you can see, after importing and instantiating the transformer (that is, **StandardScaler**), it needs to be fit to the data to then effectively transform it:

```
X_test = scaler.transform(X_test)
```

The advantage of the transformer is that once it has been applied to the training dataset, it stores the values used for transforming the training data; this can be used to transform the test dataset to the same distribution, as seen in the preceding snippet.

In conclusion, we discussed one of the main benefits of using scikit-learn, which is its API. This API follows a consistent structure that makes it easy for non-experts to apply ML algorithms.

To model an algorithm on scikit-learn, the first step is to instantiate the model's class and fit it to the input data using an estimator, which is usually done by calling the **fit()** method of the class. Finally, once the model has been trained, it is possible to predict new values using the predictor by calling the **predict()** method of the class.

Additionally, scikit-learn also has a transformer interface that allows you to transform data as needed. This is useful for performing preprocessing methods over the training data, which can then also be used to transform the testing data to follow the same distribution.

SUPERVISED AND UNSUPERVISED LEARNING

ML is divided into two main categories: supervised and unsupervised learning.

SUPERVISED LEARNING

Supervised learning consists of understanding the relationship between a given set of features and a target value, also known as a **label** or **class**. For instance, it can be used for modeling the relationship between a person's demographic information and their ability to pay loans, as shown in the following table:

Age	Sex	Education level	Income level	Marital status	Previous loan paid
30	Female	College	$97,000	Single	Yes
53	Male	High school	$80,000	Single	No
26	Male	Masters	$157,000	Married	Yes
35	Female	None	$55,000	Married	No
44	Female	Undergraduate	$122,000	Single	Yes

Figure 1.18: The relationship between a person's demographic information and the ability to pay loans

Models trained to foresee these relationships can then be applied to predict labels for new data. As we can see from the preceding example, a bank that builds such a model can then input data from loan applicants to determine if they are likely to pay back the loan.

These models can be further divided into classification and regression tasks, which are explained as follows.

Classification tasks are used to build models out of data with discrete categories as labels; for instance, a classification task can be used to predict whether a person will pay a loan. You can have more than two discrete categories, such as predicting the ranking of a horse in a race, but they must be a finite number.

Most classification tasks output the prediction as the probability of an instance to belong to each output label. The assigned label is the one with the highest probability, as can be seen in the following diagram:

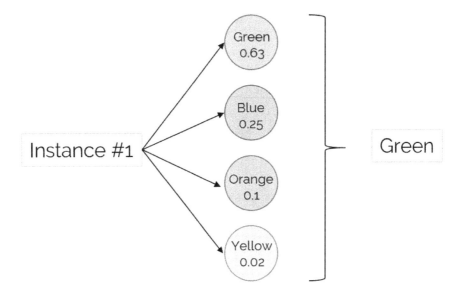

Figure 1.19: An illustration of a classification algorithm

Some of the most common classification algorithms are as follows:

- **Decision trees**: This algorithm follows a tree-like architecture that simulates the decision process following a series of decisions, considering one variable at a time.

- **Naïve Bayes classifier**: This algorithm relies on a group of probabilistic equations based on Bayes' theorem, which assumes independence among features. It has the ability to consider several attributes.

- **Artificial neural networks** (**ANNs**): These replicate the structure and performance of a biological neural network to perform pattern recognition tasks. An ANN consists of interconnected neurons, laid out with a set architecture. They pass information to one another until a result is achieved.

Regression tasks, on the other hand, are used for data with continuous quantities as labels; for example, a regression task can be used for predicting house prices. This means that the value is represented by a quantity and not by a set of possible outputs. Output labels can be of integer or float types:

- The most popular algorithm for regression tasks is **linear regression**. It consists of only one independent feature (x) whose relationship with its dependent feature (y) is linear. Due to its simplicity, it is often overlooked, even though it performs very well for simple data problems.

- Other, more complex, regression algorithms include **regression trees** and **support vector regression**, as well as **ANNs** once again.

UNSUPERVISED LEARNING

Unsupervised learning consists of fitting the model to the data without any relationship with an output label, also known as unlabeled data. This means that algorithms in this category try to understand the data and find patterns in it. For instance, unsupervised learning can be used to understand the profile of people belonging to a neighborhood, as shown in the following diagram:

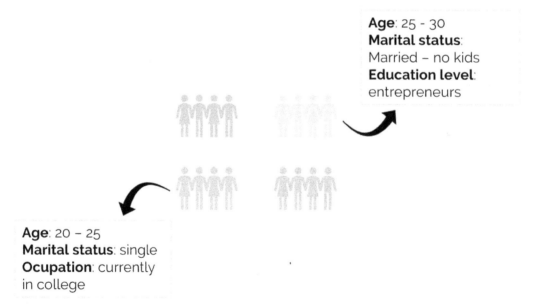

Figure 1.20: An illustration of how unsupervised algorithms can be used
to understand the profiles of people

When applying a predictor to these algorithms, no target label is given as output. The prediction, which is only available for some models, consists of placing the new instance into one of the subgroups of data that have been created. Unsupervised learning is further divided into different tasks, but the most popular one is clustering, which will be discussed next.

Clustering tasks involve creating groups of data (clusters) while complying with the condition that instances from one group differ visibly from the instances within the other groups. The output of any clustering algorithm is a label, which assigns the instance to the cluster of that label:

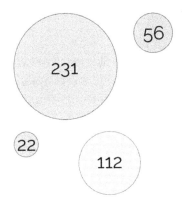

Figure 1.21: A diagram representing clusters of multiple sizes

The preceding diagram shows a group of clusters, each of a different size, based on the number of instances that belong to each cluster. Considering this, even though clusters do not need to have the same number of instances, it is possible to set the minimum number of instances per cluster to avoid overfitting the data into tiny clusters of very specific data.

Some of the most popular clustering algorithms are as follows:

- **k-means**: This focuses on separating the instances into n clusters of equal variance by minimizing the sum of the squared distances between two points.

- **Mean-shift clustering**: This creates clusters by using centroids. Each instance becomes a candidate for centroid to be the mean of the points in that cluster.

- **Density-Based Spatial Clustering of Applications with Noise (DBSCAN)**: This determines clusters as areas with a high density of points, separated by areas with low density.

SUMMARY

ML consists of constructing models that are able to convert data into knowledge that can be used to make decisions, some of which are based on complicated mathematical concepts to understand data. Scikit-learn is an open source Python library that is meant to facilitate the process of applying these models to data problems, without much complex math knowledge required.

This chapter explained the key steps of preprocessing your input data, from separating the features from the target, to dealing with messy data and rescaling the values of the data. All these steps should be performed before diving into training a model as they help to improve the training times, as well as the performance of the models.

Next, the different components of the scikit-learn API were explained: the estimator, the predictor, and the transformer. Finally, this chapter covered the difference between supervised and unsupervised learning, and the most popular algorithms of each type of learning were introduced.

With all of this in mind, in the next chapter, we will focus on detailing the process of implementing an unsupervised algorithm for a real-life dataset.

2

UNSUPERVISED LEARNING — REAL-LIFE APPLICATIONS

OVERVIEW

This chapter explains the concept of clustering in machine learning. It explains three of the most common clustering algorithms, with a hands-on approximation to solve a real-life data problem. By the end of this chapter, you should have a firm understanding of how to create clusters out of a dataset using the k-means, mean-shift, and DBSCAN algorithms, as well as the ability to measure the accuracy of those clusters.

INTRODUCTION

In the previous chapter, we learned how to represent data in a tabular format, created features and target matrices, pre-processed data, and learned how to choose the algorithm that best suits the problem at hand. We also learned how the scikit-learn API works and why it is easy to use, as well as the difference between supervised and unsupervised learning.

This chapter focuses on the most important task in the field of unsupervised learning: clustering. Consider a situation in which you are a store owner wanting to make a targeted social media campaign to promote selected products to certain customers. Using clustering algorithms, you would be able to create subgroups of your customers, allowing you to profile those subgroups and target them accordingly. The main objective of this chapter is to solve a case study, where you will implement three different unsupervised learning solutions. These different applications serve to demonstrate the uniformity of the scikit-learn API, as well as to explain the steps taken to solve machine learning problems. By the end of this chapter, you will be able to understand the use of unsupervised learning to comprehend data in order to make informed decisions.

CLUSTERING

Clustering is a type of unsupervised learning technique where the objective is to arrive at conclusions based on the patterns found within unlabeled input data. This technique is mainly used to segregate large data into subgroups in order to make informed decisions.

For instance, from a large list of restaurants in a city, it would be useful to segregate the data into subgroups (clusters) based on the type of food, quantity of clients, and style of experience, in order to be able to offer each cluster a service that's been configured to its specific needs.

Clustering algorithms divide the data points into *n* number of clusters so that the data points in the same cluster have similar features, whereas they differ significantly from the data points in other clusters.

CLUSTERING TYPES

Clustering algorithms can classify data points using a methodology that is either **hard** or **soft**. The former designates data points completely to a cluster, whereas the latter method calculates the probability of each data point belonging to each cluster. For example, for a dataset containing customer's past orders that are divided into eight subgroups (clusters), hard clustering occurs when each customer is placed inside one of the eight clusters. On the other hand, soft clustering assigns each customer a probability of belonging to each of the eight clusters.

Considering that clusters are created based on the similarity between data points, clustering algorithms can be further divided into several groups, depending on the set of rules used to measure similarity. Four of the most commonly known sets of rules are explained as follows:

- **Connectivity-based models**: This model's approach to similarity is based on proximity in a data space. The creation of clusters can be done by assigning all data points to a single cluster and then partitioning the data into smaller clusters as the distance between data points increases. Likewise, the algorithm can also start by assigning each data point an individual cluster, and then aggregating data points that are close by. An example of a connectivity-based model is hierarchical clustering.

- **Density-based models**: As the name suggests, these models define clusters by their density in the data space. This means that areas with a high density of data points will become clusters, which are typically separated from one another by low-density areas. An example of this is the DBSCAN algorithm, which will be covered later in this chapter.

- **Distribution-based models**: Models that fall into this category are based on the probability that all the data points from a cluster follow the same distribution, such as a Gaussian distribution. An example of such a model is the Gaussian Mixture algorithm, which assumes that all data points come from a mixture of a finite number of Gaussian distributions.

- **Centroid-based models**: These models are based on algorithms that define a centroid for each cluster, which is updated constantly by an iterative process. The data points are assigned to the cluster where their proximity to the centroid is minimized. An example of such a model is the k-means algorithm, which will be discussed later in this chapter.

In conclusion, data points are assigned to clusters based on their similarity to each other and their difference from data points in other clusters. This classification into clusters can be either absolute or variably distributed by determining the probability of each data point belonging to each cluster.

Moreover, there is no fixed set of rules to determine similarity between data points, which is why different clustering algorithms use different rules. Some of the most commonly known sets of rules are connectivity-based, density-based, distribution-based, and centroid-based.

APPLICATIONS OF CLUSTERING

As with all machine learning algorithms, clustering has many applications in different fields, some of which are as follows:

- **Search engine results**: Clustering can be used to generate search engine results containing keywords that are approximate to the keywords searched by the user and ordered as per the search result with greater similarity. Consider Google as an example; it uses clustering not only for retrieving results but also for suggesting new possible searches.

- **Recommendation programs**: It can also be used in recommendation programs that cluster together, for instance, people that fall into a similar profile, and then make recommendations based on the products that each member of the cluster has bought. Consider Amazon, for example, which recommends more items based on your purchase history and the purchases of similar users.

- **Image recognition**: This is where clusters are used to group images that are considered to be similar. For instance, Facebook uses clustering to help suggest who is present in a picture.

- **Market segmentation**: Clustering can also be used for market segmentation to divide a list of prospects or clients into subgroups in order to provide a customized experience or product. For example, Adobe uses clustering analysis to segment customers in order to target them differently by recognizing those who are more willing to spend money.

The preceding examples demonstrate that clustering algorithms can be used to solve different data problems in different industries, with the primary purpose of understanding large amounts of historical data that, in some cases, can be used to classify new instances.

EXPLORING A DATASET – WHOLESALE CUSTOMERS DATASET

As part of the process of learning the behavior and applications of clustering algorithms, the following sections of this chapter will focus on solving a real-life data problem using the Wholesale Customers dataset, which is available at the UC Irvine Machine Learning Repository.

> **NOTE**
>
> Datasets in repositories may contain raw, partially pre-processed, or pre-processed data. To use any of these datasets, ensure that you read the specifications of the data that's available to understand the process that needs to be followed to model the data effectively, or whether it is the right dataset for your purpose.
>
> For instance, the current dataset is an extract from a larger dataset, as per the following citation:
>
> The dataset originates from a larger database referred on: Abreu, N. (2011). Analise do perfil do cliente Recheio e desenvolvimento de um sistema promocional. Mestrado em Marketing, ISCTE-IUL, Lisbon.

In the following section, we will analyze the contents of the dataset, which will then be used in *Activity 2.01, Using Data Visualization to Aid the Pre-processing Process*. To download a dataset from the UC Irvine Machine Learning Repository, perform the following steps:

1. Access the following link: http://archive.ics.uci.edu/ml/datasets/Wholesale+customers.

2. Below the dataset's title, find the download section and click on **Data Folder**.

3. Click on the **`Wholesale Customers data.csv`** file to trigger the download and save the file in the same path as that of your current Jupyter Notebook.

> **NOTE**
>
> You can also access it by going to this book's GitHub repository:
> https://packt.live/3c3hfKp

UNDERSTANDING THE DATASET

Each step will be explained generically and will then be followed by an explanation of its application in the current case study (the Wholesale Customers dataset):

1. First of all, it is crucial to understand the way in which data is presented by the person who's responsible for gathering and maintaining it.

   Considering that the dataset of the case study was obtained from an online repository, the format in which it is presented must be understood. The Wholesale Customers dataset consists of a snippet of historical data of clients from a wholesale distributor. It contains a total of 440 instances (each row) and eight features (each column).

2. Next, it is important to determine the purpose of the study, which is dependent on the data that's available. Even though this might seem like a redundant statement, many data problems become problematic because the researcher does not have a clear view of the purpose of the study, and hence the pre-processing methodology, the model, and the performance metrics are chosen incorrectly.

   The purpose of using clustering algorithms on the Wholesale Customers dataset is to understand the behavior of each customer. This will allow you to group customers with similar behaviors into one cluster. The behavior of a customer will be defined by how much they spent on each category of product, as well as the channel and the region where they bought products.

3. Subsequently explore all the features that are available. This is mainly done for two reasons: first, to rule out features that are considered to be of low relevance based on the purpose of the study or that are considered to be redundant, and second, to understand the way the values are presented to determine some of the pre-processing techniques that may be needed.

The current case study has eight features, each one of which is considered to be relevant to the purpose of the study. Each feature is explained in the following table:

Variable	Meaning	Type	Relevance
FRESH	Annual spending* on Fresh products	Continuous	
MILK	Annual spending* on Dairy	Continuous	
GROCERY	Annual spending* on Grocery products	Continuous	These features help to identify the combination of categories that sell together based on the spending
FROZEN	Annual spending* on Frozen products	Continuous	
DETERGENTS_PA PER	Annual spending* on Detergents and paper	Continuous	
DELICATESSEN	Delicatessen products	Continuous	
CHANNEL	Customer's sales channel	Nominal**	Both features help define users based on their purchasing habits by region and sales channel
REGION	Customer's region	Nominal**	

* Annual spending measured in monetary units.
** The author of the dataset converted the nominal features into their numeric representation.

Figure 2.1: A table explaining the features in the case study

In the preceding table, no features are to be dismissed, and nominal (categorical) features have already been handled by the author of the dataset.

As a summary, the first thing to do when choosing a dataset or being handed one is to understand the characteristics that are visible at first glance, which involves recognizing the information available, then determining the purpose of the project, and finally revising the features to select those that will be part of the study. After this, the data can be visualized so that it can be understood before it's pre-processed.

DATA VISUALIZATION

Once data has been revised to ensure that it can be used for the desired purpose, it is time to load the dataset and use data visualization to further understand it. Data visualization is not a requirement for developing a machine learning project, especially when dealing with datasets with hundreds or thousands of features. However, it has become an integral part of machine learning, mainly for visualizing the following:

- Specific features that are causing trouble (for example, those that contain many missing or outlier values) and how to deal with them.

- The results from the model, such as the clusters that have been created or the number of predicted instances for each labeled category.

- The performance of the model, in order to see the behavior along different iterations.

Data visualization's popularity in the aforementioned tasks can be explained by the fact that the human brain processes information easily when it is presented as charts or graphs, which allows us to have a general understanding of the data. It also helps us to identify areas that require attention, such as outliers.

LOADING THE DATASET USING PANDAS

One way of storing a dataset to easily manage it is by using pandas DataFrames. These work as two-dimensional size-mutable matrices with labeled axes. They facilitate the use of different pandas functions to modify the dataset for pre-processing purposes.

Most datasets found in online repositories or gathered by companies for data analysis are in **Comma-Separated Values** (**CSV**) files. CSV files are text files that display the data in the form of a table. Columns are separated by commas (,) and rows are on separate lines:

```
Channel,Region,Fresh,Milk,Grocery,Frozen,Detergents_Paper,Delicassen
2,3,12669,9656,7561,214,2674,1338
2,3,7057,9810,9568,1762,3293,1776
2,3,6353,8808,7684,2405,3516,7844
1,3,13265,1196,4221,6404,507,1788
2,3,22615,5410,7198,3915,1777,5185
2,3,9413,8259,5126,666,1795,1451
```

Figure 2.2: A screenshot of a CSV file

Loading a dataset stored in a CSV file and placing it into a DataFrame is extremely easy with the pandas **read_csv()** function. It receives the path to your file as an argument.

> ### NOTE
>
> When datasets are stored in different forms of files, such as in Excel or SQL databases, use the pandas **read_xlsx()** or **read_sql()** function, respectively.

The following code shows how to load a dataset using **pandas**:

```
import pandas as pd
file_path = "datasets/test.csv"
data = pd.read_csv(file_path)
print(type(data))
```

First of all, pandas is imported. Next, the path to the file is defined in order to input it into the **read_csv()** function. Finally, the type of the **data** variable is printed to verify that a Pandas DataFrame has been created.

The output is as follows:

```
<class 'pandas.core.frame.DataFrame'>
```

As shown in the preceding snippet, the variable named **data** is of a pandas DataFrame.

VISUALIZATION TOOLS

There are different open source visualization libraries available, from which seaborn and matplotlib stand out. In the previous chapter, seaborn was used to load and display data; however, from this section onward, matplotlib will be used as our visualization library of choice. This is mainly because seaborn is built on top of matplotlib with the sole purpose of introducing a couple of plot types and to improve the format of the displays. Therefore, once you've learned about matplotlib, you will also be able to import seaborn to improve the visual quality of your plots.

> **NOTE**
>
> For more information about the seaborn library, visit the following link: https://seaborn.pydata.org/.

In general terms, matplotlib is an easy-to-use Python library that prints 2D quality figures. For simple plotting, the **pyplot** model of the library will suffice.

Some of the most commonly used plot types are explained in the following table:

Plot Type	Definition	Function	Visual Representation
Histograms	Display the distribution of continuous data	plt.hist()	
Scatter plots	Display values for two variables using Cartesian coordinates	plt.scatter()	
Bar charts	Represent variables using bars, with heights proportional to the values they represent	plt.bar()	
Pie charts	A circular representation that displays proportions	plt.pie()	

Figure 2.3: A table listing the commonly used plot types (*)

The functions in the third column can be used after importing matplotlib and its **pyplot** model.

> **NOTE**
>
> Access matplotlib's documentation regarding the type of plot that you wish to use at https://matplotlib.org/ so that you can play around with the different arguments and functions that you can use to edit the result of your plot.

EXERCISE 2.01: PLOTTING A HISTOGRAM OF ONE FEATURE FROM THE CIRCLES DATASET

In this exercise, we will be plotting a histogram of one feature from the circles dataset. Perform the following steps to complete this exercise:

> **NOTE**
>
> Use the same Jupyter Notebook for all the exercises within this chapter. The **circles.csv** file is available at https://packt.live/2xRg3ea.
>
> For all the exercises and activities within this chapter, you will need to have Python 3.7, matplotlib, NumPy, Jupyter, and pandas installed on your system.

1. Open a Jupyter Notebook to implement this exercise.

2. First, import all of the libraries that you are going to be using by typing the following code:

```
import pandas as pd
import numpy as np
import matplotlib.pyplot as plt
```

The **pandas** library is used to save the dataset into a DataFrame, **matplotlib** is used for visualization, and NumPy is used in later exercises of this chapter, but since the same Notebook will be used, it has been imported here.

3. Load the circles dataset by using Pandas' **read_csv** function. Type in the following code:

```
data = pd.read_csv("circles.csv")
plt.scatter(data.iloc[:,0], data.iloc[:,1])
plt.show()
```

A variable named **data** is created to store the circles dataset. Finally, a scatter plot is drawn to display the data points in a data space, where the first element is the first column of the dataset and the second element is the second column of the dataset, creating a two-dimensional plot:

> **NOTE**
>
> The Matplotlib's **show()** function is used to trigger the display of the plot, considering that the preceding lines only create it. When programming in Jupyter Notebooks, using the **show()** function is not required, but it is good practice to use it since, in other programming environments, it is required to use the function to be able to display the plots. This will also allow flexibility in the code. Also, in Jupyter Notebooks, this function results in a much cleaner output.

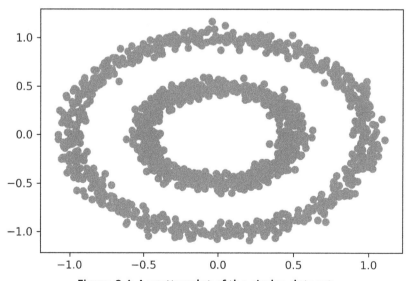

Figure 2.4: A scatter plot of the circles dataset

The final output is a dataset with two features and 1,500 instances. Here, the dot represents a data point (an observation), where the location is marked by the values of each of the features of the dataset.

4. Create a histogram out of one of the two features. Use slicing to select the feature that you wish to plot:

```
plt.hist(data.iloc[:,0])
plt.show()
```

The plot will look similar to the one shown in the following graph:

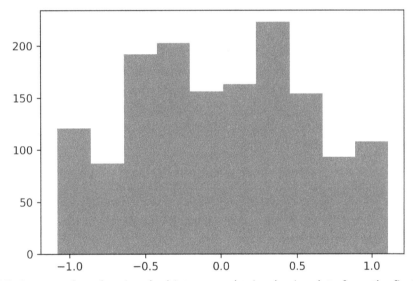

Figure 2.5: A screenshot showing the histogram obtained using data from the first feature

NOTE

To access the source code for this specific section, please refer to https://packt.live/2xRg3ea.

You can also run this example online at https://packt.live/2N0L0RJ. You must execute the entire Notebook in order to get the desired result.

You have successfully created a scatter plot and a histogram using matplotlib. Similarly, different plot types can be created using matplotlib.

In conclusion, visualization tools help you better understand the data that's available in a dataset, the results from a model, and the performance of the model. This happens because the human brain is receptive to visual forms, instead of large files of data.

Matplotlib has become one of the most commonly used libraries to perform data visualization. Among the different plot types that the library supports, there are histograms, bar charts, and scatter plots.

ACTIVITY 2.01: USING DATA VISUALIZATION TO AID THE PRE-PROCESSING PROCESS

The marketing team of your company wants to know about the different profiles of the clients so that it can focus its marketing effort on the individual needs of each profile. To do so, it has provided your team with a list of 440 pieces of previous sales data. Your first task is to pre-process the data. You will present your findings using data visualization techniques in order to help your colleagues understand the decisions you took in that process. You should load a CSV dataset using pandas and use data visualization tools to help with the pre-processing process. The following steps will guide you on how to do this:

1. Import all the required elements to load the dataset and pre-process it.

2. Load the previously downloaded dataset by using Pandas' **read_csv()** function, given that the dataset is stored in a CSV file. Store the dataset in a pandas DataFrame named **data**.

3. Check for missing values in your DataFrame. If present, handle the missing values and support your decision with data visualization.

> **NOTE**
>
> Use **data.isnull().sum()** to check for missing values in the entire dataset at once, as we learned in the previous chapter.

4. Check for outliers in your DataFrame. If present, handle the outliers and support your decision with data visualization.

> **NOTE**
>
> Mark all the values that are three standard deviations away from the mean as outliers.

5. Rescale the data using the formula for normalization or standardization.

> **NOTE**
>
> Standardization tends to work better for clustering purposes. Note that you can find the solution to this activity on page 216.

Expected output: Upon checking the DataFrame, you should find no missing values in the dataset and six features with outliers.

K-MEANS ALGORITHM

The k-means algorithm is used to model data without a labeled class. It involves dividing the data into *K* number of subgroups. The classification of data points into each group is done based on similarity, as explained previously (refer to the *Clustering Types* section), which, for this algorithm, is measured by the distance from the center (centroid) of the cluster. The final output of the algorithm is each data point linked to the cluster it belongs to and the centroid of that cluster, which can be used to label new data in the same clusters.

The centroid of each cluster represents a collection of features that can be used to define the nature of the data points that belong there.

UNDERSTANDING THE ALGORITHM

The k-means algorithm works through an iterative process that involves the following steps:

1. Based on the number of clusters defined by the user, the centroids are generated either by setting initial estimates or by randomly choosing them from the data points. This step is known as *initialization*.

2. All the data points are assigned to the nearest cluster in the data space by measuring their respective distances from the centroid, known as the assignment step. The objective is to minimize the squared Euclidean distance, which can be defined by the following formula:

```
min dist(c,x)²
```

Here, **c** represents a centroid, **x** refers to a data point, and **dist()** is the Euclidean distance.

3. Centroids are calculated again by computing the mean of all the data points belonging to a cluster. This step is known as the *update step*.

Steps 2 and *3* are repeated in an iterative process until a criterion is met. This criterion can be as follows:

- The number of iterations defined.

- The data points do not change from cluster to cluster.

- The Euclidean distance is minimized.

The algorithm is set to always arrive at a result, even though this result may converge to a local or a global optimum.

The k-means algorithm receives several parameters as inputs to run the model. The most important ones to consider are the initialization method (`init`) and the number of clusters (`K`).

> **NOTE**
>
> To check out the other parameters of the k-means algorithm in the scikit-learn library, visit the following link: http://scikit-learn.org/stable/modules/generated/sklearn.cluster.KMeans.html.

INITIALIZATION METHODS

An important input of the algorithm is the initialization method to be used to generate the initial centroids. The initialization methods allowed by the scikit-learn library are explained as follows:

- **`k-means++`**: This is the default option. Centroids are chosen randomly from the set of data points, considering that centroids must be far away from one another. To achieve this, the method assigns a higher probability of being a centroid to those data points that are farther away from other centroids.

- **`random`**: This method chooses K observations randomly from the data points as the initial centroids.

CHOOSING THE NUMBER OF CLUSTERS

As we discussed previously, the number of clusters that the data is to be divided into is set by the user; hence, it is important to choose the number of clusters appropriately.

One of the metrics that's used to measure the performance of the k-means algorithm is the mean distance of the data points from the centroid of the cluster that they belong to. However, this measure can be counterproductive as the higher the number of clusters, the smaller the distance between the data points and its centroid, which may result in the number of clusters (K) matching the number of data points, thereby harming the purpose of clustering algorithms.

To avoid this, you can plot the average distance between the data points and the cluster centroid against the number of clusters. The appropriate number of clusters corresponds to the breaking point of the plot, where the rate of decrease drastically changes. In the following diagram, the dotted circle represents the ideal number of clusters:

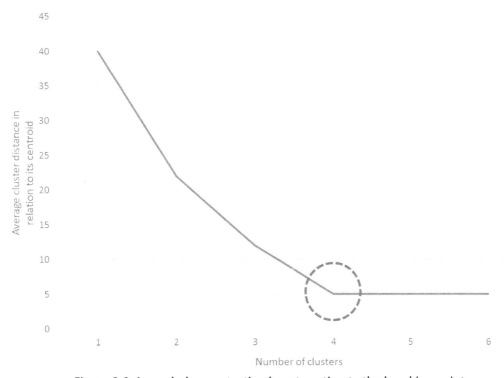

Figure 2.6: A graph demonstrating how to estimate the breaking point

EXERCISE 2.02: IMPORTING AND TRAINING THE K-MEANS ALGORITHM OVER A DATASET

The following exercise will be performed using the same dataset from the previous exercise. Considering this, use the same Jupyter Notebook that you used to develop the previous exercise. Perform the following steps to complete this exercise:

1. Open the Jupyter Notebook that you used for the previous exercise. Here, you should have imported all the required libraries and stored the dataset in a variable named **data**.

2. Import the k-means algorithm from scikit-learn as follows:

```
from sklearn.cluster import KMeans
```

3. To choose the value for K (that is, the ideal number of clusters), calculate the average distance of data points from their cluster centroid in relation to the number of clusters. Use 20 as the maximum number of clusters for this exercise. The following is a snippet of the code for this:

```
ideal_k = []
for i in range(1,21):
    est_kmeans = KMeans(n_clusters=i, random_state=0)
    est_kmeans.fit(data)
    ideal_k.append([i,est_kmeans.inertia_])
```

> **NOTE**
>
> The **random_state** argument is used to ensure reproducibility of results by making sure that the random initialization of the algorithm remains constant.

First, create the variables that will store the values as an array and name it **ideal_k**. Next, perform a **for** loop that starts at one cluster and goes as high as desired (considering that the maximum number of clusters must not exceed the total number of instances).

For the previous example, there was a limitation of a maximum of 20 clusters to be created. As a consequence of this limitation, the **for** loop goes from 1 to 20 clusters.

> **NOTE**
>
> Remember that **range ()** is an upper bound exclusive function, meaning that the range will go as far as one value below the upper bound. When the upper bound is 21, the range will go as far as 20.

Inside the **for** loop, instantiate the algorithm with the number of clusters to be created, and then fit the data to the model. Next, append the pairs of data (number of clusters, average distance to the centroid) to the list named **ideal_k**.

The average distance to the centroid does not need to be calculated as the model outputs it under the **inertia_** attribute, which can be called out as **[model_name].inertia_**.

4. Convert the **ideal_k** list into a NumPy array so that it can be plotted. Use the following code snippet:

```
ideal_k = np.array(ideal_k)
```

5. Plot the relations that you calculated in the preceding steps to find the ideal *K* to input to the final model:

```
plt.plot(ideal_k[:,0],ideal_k[:,1])
plt.show()
```

The output is as follows:

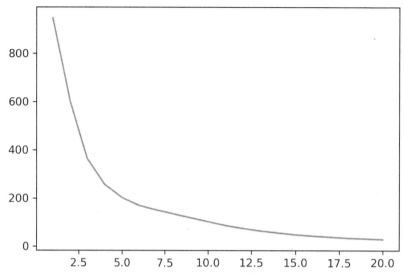

Figure 2.7: A screenshot showing the output of the plot function used

In the preceding plot, the *x-axis* represents the number of clusters, while the *y-axis* refers to the calculated average distance of each point in a cluster from their centroid.

The breaking point of the plot is around **5**.

6. Train the model with **K=5**. Use the following code:

```
est_kmeans = KMeans(n_clusters=5, random_state=0)
est_kmeans.fit(data)
pred_kmeans = est_kmeans.predict(data)
```

The first line instantiates the model with **5** as the number of clusters. Then, the data is fit to the model. Finally, the model is used to assign a cluster to each data point.

7. Plot the results from the clustering of data points into clusters:

```
plt.scatter(data.iloc[:,0], data.iloc[:,1], c=pred_kmeans)
plt.show()
```

The output is as follows:

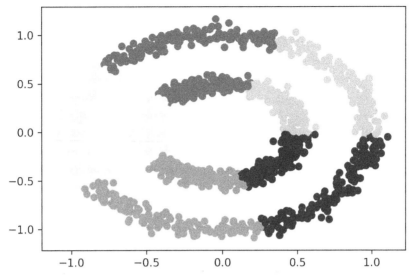

Figure 2.8: A screenshot showing the output of the plot function used

Since the dataset only contains two features, each feature is passed as input to the scatter plot function, meaning that each feature is represented by an axis. Additionally, the labels that were obtained from the clustering process are used as the colors to display the data points. Thus, each data point is located in the data space based on the values of both features, and the colors represent the clusters that were formed.

> **NOTE**
>
> For datasets with over two features, the visual representation of clusters is not as explicit as that shown in the preceding screenshot. This is mainly because the location of each data point (observation) in the data space is based on the collection of all of its features, and visually, it is only possible to display up to three features.

You have successfully imported and trained the k-means algorithm.

> **NOTE**
>
> To access the source code for this exercise, please refer to
> https://packt.live/30GXWE1.
>
> You can also run this example online at https://packt.live/2B6N1c3.
> You must execute the entire Notebook in order to get the desired result.

In conclusion, the k-means algorithm seeks to divide the data into K number of clusters, K being a parameter set by the user. Data points are grouped together based on their proximity to the centroid of a cluster, which is calculated by an iterative process.

The initial centroids are set according to the initialization method that's been defined. Then, all the data points are assigned to the clusters with the centroid closer to their location in the data space, using the Euclidean distance as a measure. Once the data points have been divided into clusters, the centroid of each cluster is recalculated as the mean of all data points. This process is repeated several times until a stopping criterion is met.

ACTIVITY 2.02: APPLYING THE K-MEANS ALGORITHM TO A DATASET

Ensure that you have completed *Activity 2.01*, *Using Data Visualization to Aid the Pre-processing Process*, before you proceed with this activity.

Continuing with the analysis of your company's past orders, you are now in charge of applying the k-means algorithm to the dataset. Using the previously loaded Wholesale Customers dataset, apply the k-means algorithm to the data and classify the data into clusters. Perform the following steps to complete this activity:

1. Open the Jupyter Notebook that you used for the previous activity. There, you should have imported all the required libraries and performed the necessary steps to pre-process the dataset.

2. Calculate the average distance of the data points from their cluster centroid in relation to the number of clusters. Based on this distance, select the appropriate number of clusters to train the model.

3. Train the model and assign a cluster to each data point in your dataset. Plot the results.

> **NOTE**
>
> You can use the **subplots()** function from Matplotlib to plot two scatter graphs at a time. To learn more about this function, visit Matplotlib's documentation at the following link: https://matplotlib.org/api/_as_gen/matplotlib.pyplot.subplots.html.
>
> You can find the solution to this activity on page 220.

The visualization of clusters will differ based on the number of clusters (k) and the features to be plotted.

MEAN-SHIFT ALGORITHM

The **mean-shift algorithm** works by assigning each data point a cluster based on the density of the data points in the data space, also known as the mode in a distribution function. Contrary to the k-means algorithm, the mean-shift algorithm does not require you to specify the number of clusters as a parameter.

The algorithm works by modeling the data points as a distribution function, where high-density areas (high concentration of data points) represent high peaks. Then, the general idea is to shift each data point until it reaches its nearest peak, which becomes a cluster.

UNDERSTANDING THE ALGORITHM

The first step of the mean-shift algorithm is to represent the data points as a density distribution. To do so, the algorithm builds upon the idea of **Kernel Density Estimation** (**KDE**), which is a method that's used to estimate the distribution of a set of data:

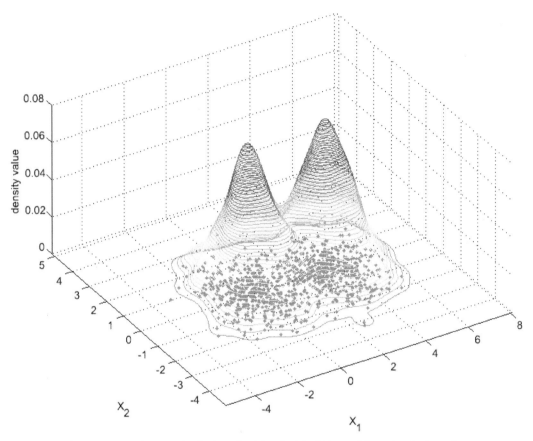

Figure 2.9: An image depicting the idea behind Kernel Density Estimation

In the preceding diagram, the dots at the bottom of the shape represent the data points that the user inputs, while the cone-shaped lines represent the estimated distribution of the data points. The peaks (high-density areas) will be the clusters. The process of assigning data points to each cluster is as follows:

1. A window of a specified size (bandwidth) is drawn around each data point.

2. The mean of the data inside the window is computed.

3. The center of the window is shifted to the mean.

Steps 2 and *3* are repeated until the data point reaches a peak, which will determine the cluster that it belongs to.

The bandwidth value should be coherent with the distribution of the data points in the dataset. For example, for a dataset normalized between 0 and 1, the bandwidth value should be within that range, while for a dataset with all values between 1,000 and 2,000, it would make more sense to have a bandwidth between 100 and 500.

In the following diagram, the estimated distribution is represented by the lines, while the data points are the dots. In each of the boxes, the data points shift to the nearest peak. All the data points in a certain peak belong to that cluster:

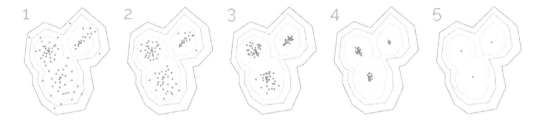

Figure 2.10: A sequence of images illustrating the working of the mean-shift algorithm

The number of shifts that a data point has to make to reach a peak depends on its bandwidth (the size of the window) and its distance from the peak.

> **NOTE**
>
> To explore all the parameters of the mean-shift algorithm in scikit-learn, visit http://scikit-learn.org/stable/modules/generated/sklearn.cluster.MeanShift.html.

EXERCISE 2.03: IMPORTING AND TRAINING THE MEAN-SHIFT ALGORITHM OVER A DATASET

The following exercise will be performed using the same dataset that we loaded in *Exercise 2.01*, *Plotting a Histogram of One Feature from the Circles Dataset*. Considering this, use the same Jupyter Notebook that you used to develop the previous exercises. Perform the following steps to complete this exercise:

1. Open the Jupyter Notebook that you used for the previous exercise.

2. Import the k-means algorithm class from scikit-learn as follows:

   ```
   from sklearn.cluster import MeanShift
   ```

3. Train the model with a bandwidth of **0.5**:

   ```
   est_meanshift = MeanShift(0.5)
   est_meanshift.fit(data)
   pred_meanshift = est_meanshift.predict(data)
   ```

   First, the model is instantiated with a bandwidth of **0.5**. Next, the model is fit to the data. Finally, the model is used to assign a cluster to each data point.

   Considering that the dataset contains values ranging from −1 to 1, the bandwidth value should not be above 1. The value of **0.5** was chosen after trying out other values, such as 0.1 and 0.9.

   > **NOTE**
   >
   > Take into account the fact that the bandwidth is a parameter of the algorithm and that, as a parameter, it can be fine-tuned to arrive at the best performance. This fine-tuning process will be covered in *Chapter 3, Supervised Learning – Key Steps*.

4. Plot the results from clustering the data points into clusters:

   ```
   plt.scatter(data.iloc[:,0], data.iloc[:,1], c=pred_meanshift)
   plt.show()
   ```

The output is as follows:

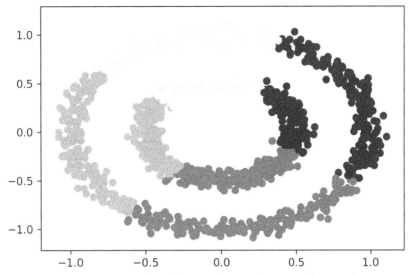

Figure 2.11: The plot obtained using the preceding code

Again, as the dataset only contains two features, both are passed as inputs to the scatter function, which become the values of the axes. Also, the labels that were obtained from the clustering process are used as the colors to display the data points.

The total number of clusters that have been created is four.

NOTE

To access the source code for this exercise, please refer to https://packt.live/37vBOOk.

You can also run this example online at https://packt.live/3e6uqM2. You must execute the entire Notebook in order to get the desired result.

You have successfully imported and trained the mean-shift algorithm.

In conclusion, the mean-shift algorithm starts by drawing the distribution function that represents the set of data points. This process consists of creating peaks in high-density areas, while leaving the areas with a low density flat.

Following this, the algorithm proceeds to classify the data points into clusters by shifting each point slowly and iteratively until it reaches a peak, which becomes its cluster.

ACTIVITY 2.03: APPLYING THE MEAN-SHIFT ALGORITHM TO A DATASET

In this activity, you will apply the mean-shift algorithm to the dataset to see which algorithm fits the data better. Therefore, using the previously loaded Wholesale Consumers dataset, apply the mean-shift algorithm to the data and classify the data into clusters. Perform the following steps to complete this activity:

1. Open the Jupyter Notebook that you used for the previous activity.

   > **NOTE**
   >
   > Considering that you are using the same Jupyter Notebook, be careful not to overwrite any previous variables.

2. Train the model and assign a cluster to each data point in your dataset. Plot the results.

   The visualization of clusters will differ based on the bandwidth and the features that have been chosen to be plotted.

   > **NOTE**
   >
   > The solution to this activity can be found on page 223.

DBSCAN ALGORITHM

The **density-based spatial clustering of applications with noise (DBSCAN)** algorithm groups together points that are close to each other (with many neighbors) and marks those points that are further away with no close neighbors as outliers.

According to this, and as its name states, the algorithm classifies data points based on the density of all data points in the data space.

UNDERSTANDING THE ALGORITHM

The DBSCAN algorithm requires two main parameters: epsilon and the minimum number of observations.

Epsilon, also known as **eps**, is the maximum distance that defines the radius within which the algorithm searches for neighbors. The **minimum number of observations**, on the other hand, refers to the number of data points required to form a high-density area (**min_samples**). However, the latter is optional in scikit-learn as the default value is set to **5**:

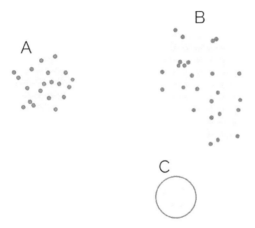

Figure 2.12: An illustration of how the DBSCAN algorithm classifies data into clusters

In the preceding diagram, the dots to the left are assigned to cluster **A**, while the dots to the upper right are assigned to cluster **B**. Moreover, the dots at the bottom right (**C**) are considered to be outliers, as well as any other data point in the data space, as they do not meet the required parameters to belong to a high-density area (that is, the minimum number of samples is not met, which, in this example, was set to **5**).

> **NOTE**
>
> Similar to the bandwidth parameter, the epsilon value should be coherent with the distribution of the data points in the dataset, considering that it represents a radius around each data point.

According to this, each data point can be classified as follows:

- **A core point**: A point that has at least the minimum number of data points within its **eps** radius.

- **A border point**: A point that is within the *eps* radius of a core point, but does not have the required number of data points within its own radius.

- **A noise point**: All points that do not meet the preceding descriptions.

> **NOTE**
>
> To explore all the parameters of the DBSCAN algorithm in scikit-learn, visit
> http://scikit-learn.org/stable/modules/generated/sklearn.cluster.DBSCAN.html.

EXERCISE 2.04: IMPORTING AND TRAINING THE DBSCAN ALGORITHM OVER A DATASET

This exercise discusses how to import and train the DBSCAN algorithm over a dataset. We will be using the circles dataset from the previous exercises. Perform the following steps to complete this exercise:

1. Open the Jupyter Notebook that you used for the previous exercise.

2. Import the DBSCAN algorithm class from scikit-learn as follows:

```
from sklearn.cluster import DBSCAN
```

3. Train the model with epsilon equal to **0.1**:

```
est_dbscan = DBSCAN(eps=0.1)
pred_dbscan = est_dbscan.fit_predict(data)
```

First, the model is instantiated with **eps** of **0.1**. Then, we use the **fit_predict()** function to fit the model to the data and assign a cluster to each data point. This bundled function, which includes both the **fit** and **predict** methods, is used because the DBSCAN algorithm in scikit-learn does not contain a **predict()** method alone.

Again, the value of **0.1** was chosen after trying out all other possible values.

4. Plot the results from the clustering process:

```
plt.scatter(data.iloc[:,0], data.iloc[:,1], c=pred_dbscan)
plt.show()
```

The output is as follows:

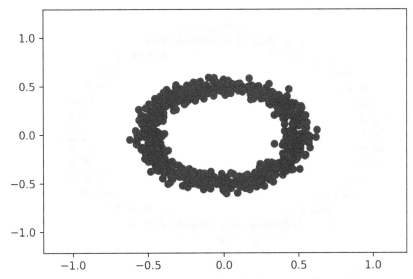

Figure 2.13: The plot obtained with the preceding code

As before, both features are passed as inputs to the scatter function. Also, the labels that were obtained from the clustering process are used as the colors to display the data points.

The total number of clusters that have been created is two.

As you can see, the total number of clusters created by each algorithm is different. This is because, as mentioned previously, each of these algorithms defines similarity differently and, as a consequence, each interprets the data differently.

Due to this, it is crucial to test different algorithms over the data to compare the results and define which one generalizes better to the data. The following topic will explore some methods that we can use to evaluate performance to help choose an algorithm.

NOTE

To access the source code for this exercise, please refer to https://packt.live/2Bcanxa.

You can also run this example online at https://packt.live/2UKHFdp.
You must execute the entire Notebook in order to get the desired result.

You have successfully imported and trained the DBSCAN algorithm.

In conclusion, the DBSCAN algorithm bases its clustering classification on the density of data points in the data space. This means that clusters are formed by data points with many neighbors. This is done by considering that core points are those that contain a minimum number of neighbors within a set radius, border points are those that are located inside the radius of a core point but do not have the minimum number of neighbors within their own radius, and noise points are those that do not meet any of the specifications.

ACTIVITY 2.04: APPLYING THE DBSCAN ALGORITHM TO THE DATASET

You will apply the DBSCAN algorithm to the dataset as well. This is basically because it is good practice to test out different algorithms when solving a data problem in order to choose the one that best fits the data, considering that there is no one model that performs well for all data problems. Using the previously loaded Wholesale Consumers dataset, apply the DBSCAN algorithm to the data and classify the data into clusters. Perform the following steps:

1. Open the Jupyter Notebook that you used for the previous activity.

2. Train the model and assign a cluster to each data point in your dataset. Plot the results.

> ### NOTE
>
> The solution to this activity can be found on page 225.

The visualization of clusters will differ based on the epsilon and the features chosen to be plotted.

EVALUATING THE PERFORMANCE OF CLUSTERS

After applying a clustering algorithm, it is necessary to evaluate how well the algorithm has performed. This is especially important when it is difficult to visually evaluate the clusters; for example, when there are several features.

Usually, with supervised algorithms, it is easy to evaluate their performance by simply comparing the prediction of each instance with its true value (class). On the other hand, when dealing with unsupervised models (such as clustering algorithms), it is necessary to pursue other strategies.

In the specific case of clustering algorithms, it is possible to evaluate performance by measuring the similarity of the data points that belong to the same cluster.

AVAILABLE METRICS IN SCIKIT-LEARN

Scikit-learn allows its users to use three different scores for evaluating the performance of unsupervised clustering algorithms. The main idea behind these scores is to measure how well-defined the cluster's edges are, instead of measuring the dispersion within a cluster. Hence, it is worth mentioning that the scores do not take into account the size of each cluster.

The two most commonly used scores for measuring unsupervised clustering tasks are explained as follows:

- The **Silhouette Coefficient Score** calculates the mean distance between each point and all the other points of a cluster (*a*), as well as the mean distance between each point and all the other points of its nearest clusters (*b*). It relates both of them according to the following equation:

```
s = (b - a) / max(a,b)
```

  The result of the score is a value between -1 and 1. The lower the value, the worse the performance of the algorithm. Values around 0 will imply overlapping of clusters. It is also important to clarify that this score does not work very well when using density-based algorithms such as DBSCAN.

- The **Calinski–Harabasz Index** was created to measure the relationship between the variance of each cluster and the variance of all clusters. More specifically, the variance of each cluster is the mean square error of each point with respect to the centroid of that cluster. On the other hand, the variance of all clusters refers to the overall inter-cluster variance.

  The higher the value of the Calinski–Harabasz Index, the better the definition and separation of the clusters. There is no acceptable cut-off value, so the performance of the algorithms using this index is evaluated through comparison, where the algorithm with the highest value is the one that performs best. As with the Silhouette Coefficient, this score does not perform well on density-based algorithms such as DBSCAN.

Unfortunately, the scikit-learn library does not contain other methods for effectively measuring the performance of density-based clustering algorithms, and although the methods mentioned here may work in some cases to measure the performance of these algorithms, when they do not, there is no other way to measure this other than via manual evaluation.

However, it is worth mentioning that there are additional performance measures in scikit-learn for cases where a ground truth label is known, known as supervised clustering; for instance, when performing clustering over a set of observations of journalism students who have already signed up for a major or a specialization area. If we were to use their demographic information as well as some student records to categorize them into clusters that represent their choice of major, it would be possible to compare the predicted classification with the actual classification.

Some of these measures are as follows:

- **Homogeneity score**: This score is based on the premise that a clustering task is homogenous if all clusters only contain data points that belong to a single class label. The output from the score is a number between 0 and 1, with 1 being a perfectly homogeneous labeling. The score is part of scikit-learn's **metrics** module, and it receives the list of ground truth clusters and the list of predicted clusters as inputs, as follows:

```
from sklearn.metrics import homogeneity_score
score = homogeneity_score(true_labels, predicted_labels)
```

- **Completeness score**: Opposite to the homogeneity score, a clustering task satisfies completeness if all data points that belong to a given class label belong to the same cluster. Again, the output measure is a number between 0 and 1, with 1 being the output for perfect completeness. This score is also part of scikit-learn's metrics modules, and it also receives the ground truth labels and the predicted ones as inputs, as follows:

```
from sklearn.metrics import completeness_score
score = completeness_score(true_labels, predicted_labels)
```

> **NOTE**
>
> To explore other measures that evaluate the performance of supervised clustering tasks, visit the following URL, under the clustering section: https://scikit-learn.org/stable/modules/classes.html#module-sklearn.metrics.

EXERCISE 2.05: EVALUATING THE SILHOUETTE COEFFICIENT SCORE AND CALINSKI–HARABASZ INDEX

In this exercise, we will learn how to calculate the two scores we discussed in the previous section that are available in scikit-learn. Perform the following steps to complete this exercise:

1. Import the Silhouette Coefficient score and the Calinski-Harabasz Index from the scikit-learn library:

```
from sklearn.metrics import silhouette_score
from sklearn.metrics import calinski_harabasz_score
```

2. Calculate the Silhouette Coefficient score for each of the algorithms we modeled in all of the previous exercises. Use the Euclidean distance as the metric for measuring the distance between points.

   The input parameters of the **silhouette_score()** function are the data, the predicted values of the model (the clusters assigned to each data point), and the distance measure:

   > **NOTE**
   >
   > The code snippet shown here uses a backslash (\ ) to split the logic across multiple lines. When the code is executed, Python will ignore the backslash, and treat the code on the next line as a direct continuation of the current line.

```
kmeans_score = silhouette_score(data, pred_kmeans, \
                                metric='euclidean')
meanshift_score = silhouette_score(data, pred_meanshift, \
                                   metric='euclidean')
dbscan_score = silhouette_score(data, pred_dbscan, \
                                metric='euclidean')
print(kmeans_score, meanshift_score, dbscan_score)
```

The first three lines call the **silhouette_score()** function over each of the models (the k-mean, the mean-shift, and the DBSCAN algorithms) by inputting the data, the predictions, and the distance measure. The last line of code prints out the score for each of the models.

The scores come to be around **0.359**, **0.3705**, and **0.1139** for the k-means, mean-shift, and DBSCAN algorithms, respectively.

You can observe that both k-means and mean-shift algorithms have similar scores, while the DBSCAN score is closer to zero. This can indicate that the performance of the first two algorithms is much better, and hence, the DBSCAN algorithm should not be considered to solve the data problem.

Nevertheless, it is important to remember that this type of score does not perform well when evaluating the DBSCAN algorithm. This is basically because as one cluster is surrounding the other one, the score can interpret that as an overlap when, in reality, the clusters are very well-defined, as is the case of the current dataset.

3. Calculate the Calinski-Harabasz index for each of the algorithms we modeled in the previous exercises in this chapter. The input parameters of the **calinski_harabasz_score()** function are the data and the predicted values of the model (the clusters assigned to each data point):

```
kmeans_score = calinski_harabasz_score(data, pred_kmeans)
meanshift_score = calinski_harabasz_score(data, pred_meanshift)
dbscan_score = calinski_harabasz_score(data, pred_dbscan)
print(kmeans_score, meanshift_score, dbscan_score)
```

Again, the first three lines apply the **calinski_harabasz_score()** function over the three models by passing the data and the prediction as inputs. The last line prints out the results.

The values come to approximately **1379.7**, **1305.14**, and **0.0017** for the k-means, mean-shift, and DBSCAN algorithms, respectively. Once again, the results are similar to the ones we obtained using the Silhouette Coefficient score, where both the k-means and mean-shift algorithms performed similarly well, while the DBSCAN algorithm did not.

Moreover, it is worth mentioning that the scale of each method (the Silhouette Coefficient score and the Calinski-Harabasz index) differs significantly, so they are not easily comparable.

> **NOTE**
>
> To access the source code for this specific section, please refer to https://packt.live/3e3Ylif.
>
> You can also run this example online at https://packt.live/2MXOQdZ. You must execute the entire Notebook in order to get the desired result.

You have successfully measured the performance of three different clustering algorithms.

In conclusion, the scores presented in this topic are a way of evaluating the performance of clustering algorithms. However, it is important to consider that the results from these scores are not definitive as their performance varies from algorithm to algorithm.

ACTIVITY 2.05: MEASURING AND COMPARING THE PERFORMANCE OF THE ALGORITHMS

You might find yourself in a situation in which you are not sure about the performance of the algorithms as it cannot be evaluated graphically. Therefore, you will have to measure the performance of the algorithms using numerical metrics that can be used to make comparisons. For the previously trained models, calculate the Silhouette Coefficient score and the Calinski-Harabasz index to measure the performance of the algorithms. The following steps provide hints regarding how you can do this:

1. Open the Jupyter Notebook that you used for the previous activity.

2. Calculate both the Silhouette Coefficient score and the Calinski-Harabasz index for all of the models that you trained previously.

The results may differ based on the choices you made during the development of the previous activities and how you initialized certain parameters in each algorithm. Nevertheless, the following results can be expected for a k-means algorithm set to divide the dataset into six clusters, a mean-shift algorithm with a bandwidth equal to 0.4, and a DBSCAN algorithm with an epsilon score of 0.8:

```
Silhouette Coefficient
K-means = 0.3515
mean-shift = 0.0933
DBSCAN = 0.1685


Calinski-Harabasz Index
K-means = 145.73
mean-shift = 112.90
DBSCAN = 42.45
```

NOTE

The solution to this activity can be found on page 226.

SUMMARY

Data problems where the input data is unrelated to the labeled output are handled using unsupervised learning models. The main objective of such data problems is to understand the data by finding patterns that, in some cases, can be generalized to new instances.

In this context, this chapter covered clustering algorithms, which work by aggregating similar data points into clusters, while separating data points that differ significantly.

Three different clustering algorithms were applied to the dataset and their performance was compared so that we can choose the one that best fits the data. Two different metrics for performance evaluation, the Silhouette Coefficient metric and the Calinski-Harabasz index, were also discussed in light of the inability to represent all of the features in a plot, and thereby graphically evaluate performance of the algorithms. However, it is important to understand that the result from the metric's evaluation is not absolute as some metrics perform better (by default) for some algorithms than for others.

In the next chapter, we will understand the steps involved in solving a data problem using supervised machine learning algorithms and learn how to perform error analysis.

3

SUPERVISED LEARNING – KEY STEPS

OVERVIEW

In this chapter, you will learn about key concepts for solving a supervised learning data problem. Starting from splitting the dataset to effectively create unbiased models that perform well on unseen data, you will learn how to measure the performance of the model in order to analyze it and take the necessary actions to improve it. By the end of this chapter, you will have a firm understanding of how to split a dataset, measure a model's performance, and perform error analysis.

INTRODUCTION

In the preceding chapter, we saw how to solve data problems using unsupervised learning algorithms and applied the concepts that we learned about to a real-life dataset. We also learned how to compare the performance of various algorithms and studied two different metrics for performance evaluation.

In this chapter, we will explore the main steps for working on a supervised machine learning problem. First, this chapter explains the different sets in which data needs to be split for training, validating, and testing your model. Next, the most common evaluation metrics will be explained. It is important to highlight that, among all the metrics available, only one should be selected as the evaluation metric of the study, and its selection should be made by considering the purpose of the study. Finally, we will learn how to perform error analysis, with the purpose of understanding what measures to take to improve the results of a model.

The previous concepts apply to both classification and regression tasks, where the former refers to problems where the output corresponds to a finite number of labels, while the latter deals with a continuous output number. For instance, a model that's created to determine whether a person will attend a meeting falls within the classification tasks group. On the other hand, a model that predicts the price of a product is solving a regression task.

SUPERVISED LEARNING TASKS

Differing from unsupervised learning algorithms, supervised learning algorithms are characterized by their ability to find relationships between a set of features and a target value (be it discrete or continuous). Supervised learning can solve two types of tasks:

- **Classification**: The objective of these tasks is to approximate a function that maps a set of features to a discrete set of outcomes. These outcomes are commonly known as class labels or categories. Each observation in the dataset should have a class label associated with it to be able to train a model that is capable of predicting such an outcome for future data.

  An example of a classification task is one that uses demographical data to determine someone's marital status.

- **Regression**: Although in regression tasks a function is also created to map a relationship between some inputs and some targets, in regression tasks, the outcome is continuous. This means that the outcome is a real value that can be an integer or a float.

An example of a regression task is using the different characteristics of a product to predict its price.

Although many algorithms can be adapted to solve both of these tasks, it is important to highlight that there are some algorithms that don't, which is why it is important to know the task that we want to perform in order to choose the algorithm accordingly.

Next, we will explore several topics that are crucial for performing any supervised learning task.

MODEL VALIDATION AND TESTING

With all the information now available online, it is easy for almost anybody to start working on a machine learning project. However, choosing the right algorithm for your data is a challenge when there are many options available. Due to this, the decision to use one algorithm over another is achieved through trial and error, where different alternatives are tested.

Moreover, the decision process to arrive at a good model covers not only the selection of the algorithm but also the tuning of its hyperparameters. To do this, a conventional approach is to divide the data into three parts (training, validation, and testing sets), which will be explained further in the next section.

DATA PARTITIONING

Data partitioning is a process involving dividing a dataset into three subsets so that each set can be used for a different purpose. This way, the development of a model is not affected by the introduction of bias. The following is an explanation of each subset:

- **Training set**: As the name suggests, this is the portion of the dataset that's used for training the model. It consists of the input data (the observations) paired with an outcome (the label class). This set can be used to train as many models as desired, using different algorithms. However, performance evaluation is not done on this set because, since this set was used to train the model, the measure would be biased.

- **Validation set**: Also known as the dev set, this set is used to perform an unbiased evaluation of each model while fine-tuning the hyperparameters. Performance evaluation is frequently done on this set of data to test different configurations of the hyperparameters.

Although the model does not learn from this data (it learns from the training set data), it is indirectly affected by the data in this set due to its participation in the process of deciding the changes to the hyperparameters.

After running different configurations of hyperparameters based on the performance of the model on the validation set, a winning model is selected for each algorithm.

- **Testing set**: This is used to perform the final evaluation of the model's performance (after training and validation) on unseen data. This helps measure the performance of the model with real-life data for future predictions.

  The testing set is also used to compare competing models. Considering that the training set was used to train different models and the validation set was used to fine-tune the hyperparameters of each model to select a winning configuration, the purpose of the testing set is to perform an unbiased comparison of the final models.

The following diagram shows the process of selecting the ideal model and using the sets mentioned previously:

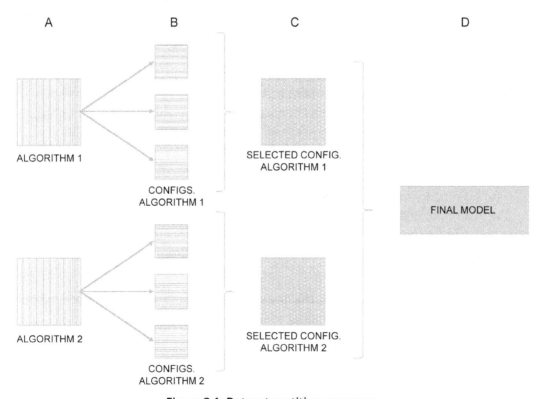

Figure 3.1: Dataset partition purposes

The sections **A–D** shown in the preceding diagram are described as follows:

- Section **A** refers to the process of training the model for the desired algorithms using the data contained in the training set.

- Section **B** represents the fine-tuning process of the hyperparameters of each model. The selection of the best configuration of hyperparameters is based on the performance of the model on the validation set.

- Section **C** shows the process of selecting the final model by comparing the final configuration of each algorithm based on its performance on the testing set.

- Finally, section **D** represents the selected model that will be applied to real-life data for prediction.

Initially, machine learning problems were solved by only partitioning data into two sets: a training and a testing set. This approach consisted of using the training set to train the model, which is the same as the approach with three sets. However, the testing set was used for fine-tuning the hyperparameters as well as for determining the ultimate performance of the algorithm.

Although this approach can also work, models that are created using this approach do not always perform equally well on unseen real-life data. This is mainly because, as mentioned previously, the use of the sets to fine-tune the hyperparameters indirectly introduces bias into the model.

Considering this, there is one way to achieve a less biased model while dividing the dataset into two sets, which is called a **cross-validation split**. We will explore this in the *Cross-Validation* section of this chapter.

SPLIT RATIO

Now that the purposes of the various sets are clear, it is important to clarify the split ratio in which data needs to be divided. Although there is no exact science for calculating the split ratio, there are a couple of things to consider when doing so:

- **Size of the dataset**: Previously, when data was not easily available, datasets contained between 100 and 100,000 instances, and the conventionally accepted split ratio was 60/20/20% for the training, validation, and testing sets, respectively.

With software and hardware improving every day, researchers can put together datasets that contain over a million instances. This capacity to gather huge amounts of data allows the split ratio to be 98/1/1%, respectively. This is mainly because the larger the dataset, the more data can be used for training a model, without compromising the amount of data left for the validation and testing sets.

- **The algorithm**: It is important to consider that some algorithms may require higher amounts of data to train a model, as is the case with neural networks. In this case, as with the preceding approaches, you should always opt for a larger training set.

  On the other hand, some algorithms do not require the validation and testing sets to be split equally. For instance, a model with fewer hyperparameters can be easily tuned, which allows the validation set to be smaller than the testing set. However, if a model has many hyperparameters, you will need to have a larger validation set.

Nevertheless, even though the preceding measures serve as a guide for splitting the dataset, it is always important to consider the distribution of your dataset and the purpose of the study. For instance, a model that is going to be used to predict an outcome on data with a different distribution than the one used to train the model, the real-life data, even if limited, must at least be a part of the testing set to make sure that the model will work for the desired purpose.

The following diagram displays the proportional partition of the dataset into three subsets. It is important to highlight that the training set must be larger than the other two, as it is the one to be used for training the model. Additionally, it is possible to observe that both the training and validation sets have an effect on the model, while the testing set is mainly used to validate the actual performance of the model with unseen data. Considering this, the training and validation sets must come from the same distribution:

Figure 3.2: Visualization of the split ratio

EXERCISE 3.01: PERFORMING A DATA PARTITION ON A SAMPLE DATASET

In this exercise, we will be performing a data partition on the **wine** dataset using the split ratio method. The partition in this exercise will be done using the three-splits approach. Follow these steps to complete this exercise:

> **NOTE**
>
> For the exercises and activities within this chapter, you will need to have Python 3.7, NumPy, Jupyter, Pandas, and scikit-learn installed on your system.

1. Open a Jupyter Notebook to implement this exercise. Import the required elements, as well as the **load_wine** function from scikit-learn's **datasets** package:

```
from sklearn.datasets import load_wine
import pandas as pd
from sklearn.model_selection import train_test_split
```

The first line imports the function that will be used to load the dataset from scikit-learn. Next, **pandas** library is imported. Finally, the **train_test_split** function is imported, which will be in charge of partitioning the dataset. The function partitions the data into two subsets (a train and a test set). As the objective of this exercise is to partition data into three subsets, the function will be used twice to achieve the desired result.

2. Load the **wine** toy dataset and store it in a variable named **data**. Use the following code snippet to do so:

```
data = load_wine()
```

The **load_wine** function loads the toy dataset provided by scikit-learn.

> **NOTE**
>
> To check the characteristics of the dataset, visit the following link: https://scikit-learn.org/stable/modules/generated/sklearn.datasets.load_wine.html.

The output from the preceding function is a dictionary-like object, which separates the features (callable as data) from the target (callable as target) into two attributes.

3. Convert each attribute (data and target) into a Pandas DataFrame to facilitate data manipulation. Print the shape of both DataFrames:

```
X = pd.DataFrame(data.data)
Y = pd.DataFrame(data.target)
print(X.shape,Y.shape)
```

The output from the **print** function should be as follows:

```
(178, 13) (178, 1)
```

Here, the values in the first parenthesis represent the shape of DataFrame **X** (known as the features matrix), while the values in the second parenthesis refer to the shape of DataFrame **Y** (known as the target matrix).

4. Perform your first split of the data using the **train_test_split** function. Use the following code snippet to do so:

```
X, X_test, Y, Y_test = train_test_split(X, Y, test_size = 0.2)
```

The inputs of the **train_test_split** function are the two matrices **(X,Y)** and the size of the test set, as a value between 0 and 1, which represents the proportion.

> **NOTE**
>
> Considering that we are dealing with a small dataset, as per the explanation in the *Split Ratio* section, we're using a split ratio of 60/20/20%. Remember that for larger datasets, the split ratio usually changes to 98/1/1%.

The outputs of the preceding function are four matrices: **X** divided into two subsets (train and test) and **Y** divided into two corresponding subsets:

```
print(X.shape, X_test.shape, Y.shape, Y_test.shape)
```

By printing the shape of all four matrices, as per the preceding code snippet, it is possible to confirm that the size of the test subset (both **X** and **Y**) is 20% of the total size of the original dataset (150 * 0.2 = 35.6) rounded to an integer, while the size of the train set is the remaining 80%:

```
(142, 13) (36, 13) (142, 1) (36, 1)
```

5. To create a validation set (dev set), we will use the **train_test_split** function to divide the train sets we obtained in the previous step. However, to obtain a dev set that's the same shape as the test set, it is necessary to calculate the proportion of the size of the test set over the size of the train set before creating a validation set. This value will be used as the **test_size** for the next step:

```
dev_size = 36/142
print(dev_size)
```

Here, **36** is the size of the test set we created in the previous step, while **142** is the size of the train set that will be further split. The result from this operation is around **0.25**, which can be verified using the **print** function.

6. Use the **train_test_split** function to divide the train set into two subsets (train and dev sets). Use the result from the operation in the previous step as the **test_size**:

```
X_train, X_dev, Y_train, Y_dev = train_test_split(X, Y, \
                                 test_size = dev_size)

print(X_train.shape, Y_train.shape, X_dev.shape, \
      Y_dev.shape, X_test.shape, Y_test.shape)
```

The output of the **print** function is as follows:

```
(106, 13) (106, 1) (36, 13) (36, 1) (36, 13) (36, 1)
```

> **NOTE**
>
> To access the source code for this specific section, please refer to https://packt.live/2AtXAWS.
>
> You can also run this example online at https://packt.live/2YECtsG.
> You must execute the entire Notebook in order to get the desired result.

You have successfully split the dataset into three subsets to develop efficient machine learning projects. Feel free to test different split ratios.

In conclusion, the split ratio to partition data is not fixed and should be decided by taking into account the amount of data available, the type of algorithm to be used, and the distribution of the data.

CROSS-VALIDATION

Cross-validation is also a procedure that's used to partition data by resampling the data that's used to train and validate the model. It consists of a parameter, K, that represents the number of groups that the dataset will be divided into.

Due to this, the procedure is also referred to as K-fold cross-validation, where K is usually replaced by a number of your choice. For instance, a model that's created using a 10-fold cross-validation procedure signifies a model where data is divided into 10 subgroups. The procedure of cross-validation is illustrated in the following diagram:

Figure 3.3: Cross-validation procedure

The preceding diagram displays the general procedure that's followed during cross-validation:

1. Data is shuffled randomly, considering that the cross-validation process is repeated.

2. Data is split into K subgroups.

3. The validation/testing set is selected as one of the subgroups that were created. The rest of the subgroups become the training set.

4. The model is trained on the training set, as usual. The model is evaluated using the validation/testing set.

5. The result from that iteration is saved. The parameters are tuned based on the results, and the process starts again by reshuffling the data. This process is repeated K number of times.

According to the preceding steps, the dataset is divided into *K* sets and the model is trained *K* times. Each time, one set is selected as the validation set and the remaining sets are used for the training process.

Cross-validation can be done using a three-split approach or a two-split one. For the former, the dataset is initially divided into training and testing sets, after which the training set is divided using cross-validation to create different configurations of training and validation sets. The latter approach, on the other hand, uses cross-validation on the entire dataset.

The popularity of cross-validation is due to its capacity to build "unbiased" models as it allows us to measure the performance of the algorithm on different segments of the dataset, which also provides us with an idea of its performance on unseen data. It is also popular because it allows you to build highly effective models out of a small dataset.

There is no exact science to choosing the value for *K*, but it is important to consider that lower values for *K* tend to decrease variance and increase bias, while higher *K* values result in the opposite behavior. Also, the lower *K* is, the less expensive the processes, which results in faster running times.

> **NOTE**
>
> The concepts of variance and bias will be explained in the *Bias, Variance, and Data Mismatch* section.

EXERCISE 3.02: USING CROSS-VALIDATION TO PARTITION THE TRAIN SET INTO A TRAINING AND A VALIDATION SET

In this exercise, we will be performing a data partition on the `wine` dataset using the cross-validation method. Follow these steps to complete this exercise:

1. Open a Jupyter Notebook to implement this exercise and import all the required elements:

```
from sklearn.datasets import load_wine
import pandas as pd
from sklearn.model_selection import train_test_split
from sklearn.model_selection import KFold
```

The last line in the preceding code imports the **KFold** class from scikit-learn, which will be used to partition the dataset.

2. Load the **wine** dataset as per the previous exercise and create the Pandas DataFrames containing the features and target matrices:

```
data = load_wine()
X = pd.DataFrame(data.data)
Y = pd.DataFrame(data.target)
```

3. Split the data into training and testing sets using the **train_test_split** function, which you learned about in the previous exercise, using a **test_size** of 0.10:

```
X, X_test, Y, Y_test = train_test_split(X, Y, \
                                        test_size = 0.10)
```

4. Instantiate the **KFold** class with a 10-fold configuration:

```
kf = KFold(n_splits = 10)
```

> **NOTE**
>
> Feel free to experiment with the values of **K** to see how the output shapes of this exercise vary.

5. Apply the **split** method to the data in **X**. This method will output the index of the instances to be used as training and validation sets. This method creates 10 different split configurations. Save the output in a variable named **splits**:

```
splits = kf.split(X)
```

Note that it is not necessary to run the **split** method on the data in **Y**, as the method only saves the index numbers, which will be the same for **X** and **Y**. The actual splitting is handled next.

6. Perform a **for** loop that will go through the different split configurations. In the loop body, create the variables that will hold the data for the training and validation sets. Use the following code snippet to do so:

```
for train_index, test_index in splits:
    X_train, X_dev = X.iloc[train_index,:], \
                     X.iloc[test_index,:]
    Y_train, Y_dev = Y.iloc[train_index,:], \
                     Y.iloc[test_index,:]
```

The **for** loop goes through **K** number of configurations. In the body of the loop, the data is split using the index numbers:

```
print(X_train.shape, Y_train.shape, X_dev.shape, \
      Y_dev.shape, X_test.shape, Y_test.shape)
```

By printing the shape of all the subsets, as per the preceding snippet, the output is as follows:

```
(144, 13) (144, 1) (16, 13) (16, 1) (18, 13) (18, 1)
```

> **NOTE**
>
> The code to train and evaluate the model should be written inside the loop body, given that the objective of the cross-validation procedure is to train and validate the model using the different split configurations.

You have successfully performed a cross-validation split on a sample dataset.

> **NOTE**
>
> To access the source code for this specific section, please refer to https://packt.live/2N0IPi0.
>
> You can also run this example online at https://packt.live/2Y290tK.
> You must execute the entire Notebook in order to get the desired result.

In conclusion, cross-validation is a procedure that's used to shuffle and split the data into training and validation sets so that the process of training and validating is done each time on a different set of data, thus achieving a model with low bias.

ACTIVITY 3.01: DATA PARTITIONING ON A HANDWRITTEN DIGIT DATASET

Your company specializes in recognizing handwritten characters. It wants to improve the recognition of digits, which is why they have gathered a dataset of 1,797 handwritten digits from 0 to 9. The images have already been converted into their numeric representation, and so they have provided you with the dataset to split it into training/validation/testing sets. You can choose to either perform conventional splitting or cross-validation. Follow these steps to complete this activity:

1. Import all the required elements to split a dataset, as well as the **load_digits** function from scikit-learn to load the **digits** dataset.

2. Load the **digits** dataset and create Pandas DataFrames containing the features and target matrices.

3. Take the conventional split approach, using a split ratio of 60/20/20%.

4. Using the same DataFrames, perform a 10-fold cross-validation split.

> **NOTE**
>
> The solution for this activity can be found on page 228. Feel free to try different parameters to arrive at different results.

EVALUATION METRICS

Model evaluation is indispensable for creating effective models that not only perform well on the data that was used to train the model but also on unseen data. The task of evaluating the model is especially easy when dealing with supervised learning problems, where there is a ground truth that can be compared against the prediction of the model.

Determining the accuracy percentage of the model is crucial for its application to unseen data that does not have a label class to compare to. For example, a model with an accuracy of 98% may allow the user to assume that the odds of having an accurate prediction are high, and hence the model should be trusted.

The evaluation of performance, as mentioned previously, should be done on the validation set (dev set) to fine-tune the model, and on the test set to determine the expected performance of the selected model on unseen data.

EVALUATION METRICS FOR CLASSIFICATION TASKS

A classification task refers to a model where the class label is a discrete value, as mentioned previously. Considering this, the most common measure to evaluate the performance of such tasks is calculating the accuracy of the model, which involves comparing the actual prediction to the real value. Even though this may be an appropriate metric in many cases, there are several others to consider as well before choosing one.

Now, we will take a look at the different performance metrics.

CONFUSION MATRIX

The **confusion matrix** is a table that contains the performance of the model, and is described as follows:

- The columns represent the instances that belong to a predicted class.

- The rows refer to the instances that actually belong to that class (ground truth).

The configuration that confusion matrices present allows the user to quickly spot the areas in which the model is having greater difficulty. Consider the following table:

Prediction / Ground truth	Pregnant	Not Pregnant
Pregnant	556	44
Not Pregnant	123	477

Figure 3.4: A confusion matrix of a classifier that predicts whether a woman is pregnant

The following can be observed from the preceding table:

- By summing up the values in the first row, it is possible to know that there are 600 observations of pregnant women. However, from those 600 observations, the model predicted 556 as pregnant, and 44 as non-pregnant. Hence, the model's ability to predict that a woman is pregnant has a correctness level of 92.6%.

- Regarding the second row, there are also 600 observations of non-pregnant women. Out of those 600, the model predicted that 123 of them were pregnant, and 477 were non-pregnant. The model successfully predicted non-pregnant women 79.5% of the time.

Based on these statements, it is possible to conclude that the model performs at its worst when classifying observations that are not pregnant.

Considering that the rows in a confusion matrix refer to the occurrence or non-occurrence of an event, and the columns refer to the model's predictions, the values in the confusion matrix can be explained as follows:

- **True positives** (**TP**): Refers to the instances that the model correctly classified the event as positive—for example, the instances correctly classified as pregnant.

- **False positives** (**FP**): Refers to the instances that the model incorrectly classified the event as positive—for example, the non-pregnant instances that were incorrectly classified as pregnant.

- **True negatives** (**TN**): Represents the instances that the model correctly classified the event as negative—for example, the instances correctly classified as non-pregnant.

- **False negatives** (**FN**): Refers to the instances that the model incorrectly classified the event as negative—for example, the pregnant instances that were incorrectly predicted as non-pregnant.

The values in the confusion matrix can be demonstrated as follows:

	Predicted: True	**Predicted: False**
Actual: True	TP	FN
Actual: False	FP	TN

Figure 3.5: A table showing confusion matrix values

ACCURACY

Accuracy, as explained previously, measures the model's ability to correctly classify all instances. Although this is considered to be one of the simplest ways of measuring performance, it may not always be a useful metric when the objective of the study is to minimize/maximize the occurrence of one class independently of its performance on other classes.

The accuracy level of the confusion matrix from *Figure 3.4* is measured as follows:

$$Accuracy = \frac{(TP + TN)}{m} = 0.8608 \approx 86\%$$

Figure 3.6: An equation showing the calculation for accuracy

Here, *m* is the total number of instances.

The **86%** accuracy refers to the overall performance of the model in classifying both class labels.

PRECISION

This metric measures the model's ability to correctly classify positive labels (the label that represents the occurrence of the event) by comparing it with the total number of instances predicted as positive. This is represented by the ratio between the *true positives* and the sum of the *true positives* and *false positives*, as shown in the following equation:

$$Precision = \frac{TP}{TP + FP}$$

Figure 3.7: An equation showing the calculation for precision

The precision metric is only applicable to binary classification tasks, where there are only two class labels (for instance, true or false). It can also be applied to multiclass tasks considering that the classes are converted into two (for instance, predicting whether a handwritten number is a 6 or any other number), where one of the classes refers to the instances that have a condition while the other refers to those that do not.

For the example in *Figure 3.4*, the precision of the model is equal to 81.8%.

RECALL

The recall metric measures the number of correctly predicted positive labels against all positive labels. This is represented by the ratio between *true positives* and the sum of *true positives* and *false negatives*:

$$Recall = \frac{TP}{TP + FN}$$

Figure 3.8: An equation showing the calculation for recall

Again, this measure should be applied to two class labels. The value of recall for the example in *Figure 3.4* is 92.6%, which, when compared to the other two metrics, represents the highest performance of the model. The decision to choose one metric or the other will depend on the purpose of the study, which will be explained in more detail later.

EXERCISE 3.03: CALCULATING DIFFERENT EVALUATION METRICS ON A CLASSIFICATION TASK

In this exercise, we will be using the breast cancer toy dataset to calculate the evaluation metrics using the scikit-learn library. Follow these steps to complete this exercise:

1. Open a Jupyter Notebook to implement this exercise and import all the required elements:

```
from sklearn.datasets import load_breast_cancer
import pandas as pd
from sklearn.model_selection import train_test_split
from sklearn import tree
from sklearn.metrics import confusion_matrix
from sklearn.metrics import accuracy_score
from sklearn.metrics import precision_score
from sklearn.metrics import recall_score
```

The fourth line imports the **tree** module from scikit-learn, which will be used to train a decision tree model on the training data in this exercise. The lines of code below that will import the different evaluation metrics that will be calculated during this exercise.

2. The breast cancer toy dataset contains the final diagnosis (malignant or benign) of the analysis of masses found in the breasts of 569 women. Load the dataset and create features and target Pandas DataFrames, as follows:

```
data = load_breast_cancer()
X = pd.DataFrame(data.data)
Y = pd.DataFrame(data.target)
```

3. Split the dataset using the conventional split approach:

```
X_train, X_test, \
Y_train, Y_test = train_test_split(X,Y, test_size = 0.1, \
                                   random_state = 0)
```

Note that the dataset is divided into two subsets (train and test sets) because the purpose of this exercise is to learn how to calculate the evaluation metrics using the scikit-learn package.

> **NOTE**
>
> The **random_state** parameter is used to set a seed that will ensure the same results every time you run the code. This guarantees that you will get the same results as the ones reflected in this exercise. Different numbers can be used as the seed; however, use the same number as suggested in the exercises and activities of this chapter to get the same results as the ones shown here.

4. First, instantiate the **DecisionTreeClassifier** class from scikit-learn's **tree** module. Next, train a decision tree on the train set. Finally, use the model to predict the class label on the test set. Use the following code to do this:

```
model = tree.DecisionTreeClassifier(random_state = 0)
model = model.fit(X_train, Y_train)
Y_pred = model.predict(X_test)
```

First, the model is instantiated using a **random_state** to set a seed. Then, the **fit** method is used to train the model using the data from the train sets (both **X** and **Y**). Finally, the **predict** method is used to trigger the predictions on the data in the test set (only **X**). The data from **Y_test** will be used to compare the predictions with the ground truth.

> **NOTE**
>
> The steps for training a supervised learning model will be explained further in *Chapter 4, Supervised Learning Algorithms: Predicting Annual Income* and *Chapter 5, Artificial Neural Networks: Predicting Annual Income*.

5. Use scikit-learn to construct a confusion matrix, as follows:

```
confusion_matrix(Y_test, Y_pred)
```

The result is as follows, where the ground truth is measured against the prediction:

```
array([[21, 1],
       [6, 29]])
```

6. Calculate the accuracy, precision, and recall of the model by comparing **Y_test** and **Y_pred**:

```
accuracy = accuracy_score(Y_test, Y_pred)
print("accuracy:", accuracy)

precision = precision_score(Y_test, Y_pred)
print("precision:", precision)

recall = recall_score(Y_test, Y_pred)
print("recall:", recall)
```

The results are displayed as follows:

```
accuracy: 0.8771
precision: 0.9666
recall: 0.8285
```

Given that the positive labels are those where the mass is malignant, it can be concluded that the instances that the model predicts as malignant have a high probability (96.6%) of being malignant, but for the instances predicted as benign, the model has a 17.15% (100%–82.85%) probability of being wrong.

> **NOTE**
>
> To access the source code for this specific section, please refer to https://packt.live/2Yw0hiu.
>
> You can also run this example online at https://packt.live/3e4rRtE.
> You must execute the entire Notebook in order to get the desired result.

You have successfully calculated evaluation metrics on a classification task.

CHOOSING AN EVALUATION METRIC

There are several metrics that can be used to measure the performance of a model on classification tasks, and selecting the right one is key to building a model that performs exceptionally well for the purpose of the study.

Previously, the importance of understanding the purpose of the study was mentioned as a useful insight to determine the pre-processing techniques that need to be performed on the dataset. Moreover, the purpose of the study is also useful to determine the ideal metric for measuring the performance of the model.

Why is the purpose of the study important for selecting the evaluation metric? Because by understanding the main goal of the study, it is possible to decide whether it is important to focus our attention on the overall performance of the model or only on one of the class labels.

For instance, a model that has been created to recognize when birds are present in a picture does not need to perform well in recognizing which other animals are present in the picture as long as it does not classify them as birds. This means that the model needs to focus on improving the performance of correctly classifying birds only.

On the other hand, for a model that has been created to recognize handwritten characters, where no one character is more important than another, the ideal metric would be the one that measures the overall accuracy of the model.

What would happen if more than one metric was selected? It would become difficult to arrive at the best performance of the model, considering that measuring two metrics simultaneously can result in needing different approaches to improve results.

EVALUATION METRICS FOR REGRESSION TASKS

Considering that regression tasks are those where the final output is continuous, without a fixed number of output labels, the comparison between the ground truth and the prediction is based on the proximity of the values rather than on them having exactly the same values. For instance, when predicting house prices, a model that predicts a value of USD 299,846 for a house valued at USD 300,000 can be considered to be a good model.

The two metrics most commonly used for evaluating the accuracy of continuous variables are the **Mean Absolute Error** (**MAE**) and the **Root Mean Squared Error** (**RMSE**), which are explained here:

- **Mean Absolute Error**: This metric measures the average absolute difference between a prediction and the ground truth, without taking into account the direction of the error. The formula to calculate the MAE is as follows:

$$MAE = \frac{1}{m} * \sum_{i=1}^{m} |y_i - \hat{y}_i|$$

Figure 3.9: An equation showing the calculation of MAE

Here, m refers to the total number of instances, y is the ground truth, and $\hat{y}$ is the predicted value.

- **Root Mean Squared Error**: This is a quadratic metric that also measures the average magnitude of error between the ground truth and the prediction. As its name suggests, the RMSE is the square root of the average of the squared differences, as shown in the following formula:

$$RMSE = \sqrt{\frac{1}{m} * \sum_{i=1}^{m} (y_i - \hat{y}_i)^2}$$

Figure 3.10: An equation showing the calculation of RMSE

Both these metrics express the average error, in a range from 0 to infinity, where the lower the value, the better the performance of the model. The main difference between these two metrics is that the MAE assigns the same weight of importance to all errors, while the RMSE squares the error, assigning higher weights to larger errors.

Considering this, the RMSE metric is especially useful in cases where larger errors should be penalized, meaning that outliers are taken into account in the measurement of performance. For instance, the RMSE metric can be used when a value that is off by 4 is more than twice as bad as being off by 2. The MAE, on the other hand, is used when a value that is off by 4 is just twice as bad as a value off by 2.

EXERCISE 3.04: CALCULATING EVALUATION METRICS ON A REGRESSION TASK

In this exercise, we will be calculating evaluation metrics on a model that was trained using linear regression. We will use the **boston** toy dataset for this purpose. Follow these steps to complete this exercise:

1. Open a Jupyter Notebook to implement this exercise and import all the required elements, as follows:

```
from sklearn.datasets import load_boston
import pandas as pd
from sklearn.model_selection import train_test_split
from sklearn import linear_model
from sklearn.metrics import mean_absolute_error
from sklearn.metrics import mean_squared_error
import numpy as np
```

The fourth line imports the **linear_model** module from scikit-learn, which will be used to train a linear regression model on the training dataset. The lines of code that follow import two performance metrics that will be evaluated in this exercise.

2. For this exercise, the **boston** toy dataset will be used. This dataset contains data about 506 house prices in Boston. Use the following code to load and split the dataset, the same as we did for the previous exercises:

```
data = load_boston()
X = pd.DataFrame(data.data)
Y = pd.DataFrame(data.target)

X_train, X_test, Y_train, Y_test = train_test_split(X,Y, \
                                   test_size = 0.1, random_state = 0)
```

3. Train a linear regression model on the train set. Then, use the model to predict the class label on the test set, as follows:

```
model = linear_model.LinearRegression()
model = model.fit(X_train, Y_train)
Y_pred = model.predict(X_test)
```

As a general explanation, the **LinearRegression** class from scikit-learn's **linear_model** module is instantiated first. Then, the **fit** method is used to train the model using the data from the train sets (both **X** and **Y**). Finally, the **predict** method is used to trigger the predictions on the data in the test set (only **X**). The data from **Y_test** will be used to compare the predictions to the ground truth.

4. Calculate both the MAE and RMSE metrics:

```
MAE = mean_absolute_error(Y_test, Y_pred)
print("MAE:", MAE)
RMSE = np.sqrt(mean_squared_error(Y_test, Y_pred))
print("RMSE:", RMSE)
```

The results are displayed as follows:

```
MAE: 3.9357
RMSE: 6.4594
```

> **NOTE**
>
> The scikit-learn library allows you to directly calculate the MSE. To calculate the RMSE, the square root of the value obtained from the **mean_squared_error()** function is calculated. By using the square root, we ensure that the values from MAE and RMSE are comparable.

From the results, it is possible to conclude that the model performs well on the test set, considering that both values are close to zero. Nevertheless, this also means that the performance can still be improved.

> **NOTE**
>
> To access the source code for this specific section, please refer to https://packt.live/2YxVXiU.
>
> You can also run this example online at https://packt.live/2N0EIqy. You must execute the entire Notebook in order to get the desired result.

You have now successfully calculated evaluation metrics on a regression task that aimed to calculate the prices of houses based on their characteristics. In the next activity, we will calculate the performance of a classification model that was created to recognize handwritten characters.

ACTIVITY 3.02: EVALUATING THE PERFORMANCE OF THE MODEL TRAINED ON A HANDWRITTEN DATASET

You continue to work on creating a model to recognize handwritten digits. The team has built a model and they want you to evaluate the performance of the model. In this activity, you will calculate different performance evaluation metrics on a trained model. Follow these steps to complete this activity:

1. Import all the required elements to load and split a dataset in order to train a model and evaluate the performance of the classification tasks.

2. Load the **digits** toy dataset from scikit-learn and create Pandas DataFrames containing the features and target matrices.

3. Split the data into training and testing sets. Use 20% as the size of the testing set.

4. Train a decision tree on the train set. Then, use the model to predict the class label on the test set.

> **NOTE**
>
> To train the decision tree, revisit *Exercise 3.04, Calculating Different Evaluation Metrics on a Classification Task.*

5. Use scikit-learn to construct a confusion matrix.

6. Calculate the accuracy of the model.

7. Calculate the precision and recall. Considering that both the precision and recall can only be calculated on binary classification problems, we'll assume that we are only interested in classifying instances as the number **6** or **any other number**.

To be able to calculate the precision and recall, use the following code to convert **Y_test** and **Y_pred** into a one-hot vector. A one-hot vector consists of a vector that only contains zeros and ones. For this activity, the 0 represents the *number 6*, while the 1 represents **any other number**. This converts the class labels (**Y_test** and **Y_pred**) into binary data, meaning that there are only two possible outcomes instead of 10 different ones.

Then, calculate the precision and recall using the new variables:

```
Y_test_2 = Y_test[:]
Y_test_2[Y_test_2 != 6] = 1
Y_test_2[Y_test_2 == 6] = 0

Y_pred_2 = Y_pred
Y_pred_2[Y_pred_2 != 6] = 1
Y_pred_2[Y_pred_2 == 6] = 0
```

You should obtain the following values as the output:

```
Accuracy = 84.72%
Precision = 98.41%
Recall = 98.10%
```

> **NOTE**
>
> The solution for this activity can be found on page 230.

ERROR ANALYSIS

Building an average model, as explained so far, is surprisingly easy through the use of the scikit-learn library. The key aspects of building an exceptional model come from the analysis and decision-making on the part of the researcher.

As we have seen so far, some of the most important tasks are choosing and pre-processing the dataset, determining the purpose of the study, and selecting the appropriate evaluation metric. After handling all of this and taking into account that a model needs to be fine-tuned in order to reach the highest standards, most data scientists recommend training a simple model, regardless of the hyperparameters, to get the study started.

Error analysis is then introduced as a very useful methodology to turn an average model into an exceptional one. As the name suggests, it consists of analyzing the errors among the different subsets of the dataset in order to target the condition that is affecting the model at a greater scale.

BIAS, VARIANCE, AND DATA MISMATCH

To understand the different conditions that may affect a machine learning model, it is important to understand what the **Bayes error** is. The Bayes error, also known as the **irreducible error**, is the lowest possible error rate that can be achieved.

Before the improvements that were made in technology and artificial intelligence, the Bayes error was considered to be the lowest possible error achievable by humans (**human error**). For instance, for a process that most humans achieve with an error rate of 0.1, but top experts achieve with an error rate of 0.05, the Bayes error would be 0.05.

However, the Bayes error has now been redefined as being the lowest possible error that machines can achieve, which is unknown considering that, as humans, we can only understand as far as human error goes. Due to this, when using the Bayes error to analyze errors, it is not possible to know the lowest limit once the model is below the human error.

The following diagram is useful for analyzing the error rates among the different sets of data and determining the condition that is affecting the model in a greater proportion. The purpose of this diagram is to find the errors that differ to a greater extent from each other so that the model can be diagnosed and improved accordingly. It is important to highlight that the value of the error for each set is calculated by subtracting the evaluation metrics (for instance, the accuracy) of that set from 100%:

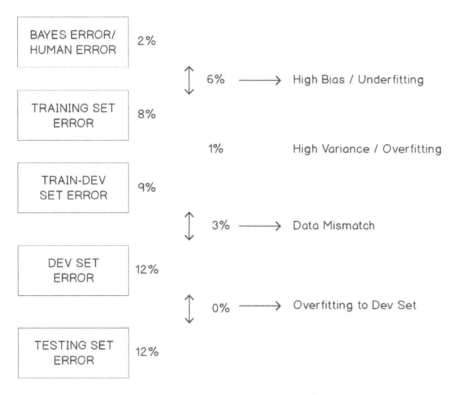

Figure 3.11: Error analysis methodology

Considering the preceding diagram, the process to perform error analysis is as follows:

1. The performance evaluation is calculated on all sets of data. This measure is used to calculate the error for each set.

2. Starting from the bottom to the top, the difference is calculated as follows:

   The dev set error (12%) is subtracted from the testing set error (12%). The resulting value (0%) is saved.

   The train-dev error (9%) is subtracted from the dev set error (12%). The resulting value (3%) is saved.

   The training set error (8%) is subtracted from the train-dev error (9%). The resulting value (1%) is saved.

   The Bayes error (2%) is subtracted from the training set error (8%). The resulting value (6%) is saved.

3. The bigger difference determines the condition that is most seriously affecting the model. In this case, the bigger difference occurs between the Bayes error and the training set error, which, as shown in the preceding diagram, determines that the model is suffering from *high bias*.

> **NOTE**
>
> The train/dev set is a combination of data in the training and the validation (dev) sets. It is usually of the same shape as the dev set and contains the same amount of data from both sets.

An explanation of each of the conditions is as follows, along with some techniques to avoid/fix them:

- **High Bias**: Also known as underfitting, this occurs when the model is not learning from the training set, which translates into the model performing poorly for all three sets (training, validation, and testing sets), as well as for unseen data.

  Underfitting is the easiest condition to detect and it usually requires changing to a different algorithm that may be a better fit for the data available. With regard to neural networks, it can typically be fixed by constructing a bigger network or by training for longer periods of time.

- **High Variance**: Also known as overfitting, this condition refers to the model's inability to perform well on data that's different than that of the training set. This basically means that the model has overfitted the training data by learning the details and outliers of the data, without making any generalizations. A model suffering from overfitting will not perform well on the dev or test sets, or on unseen data.

  Overfitting can be fixed by tuning the different hyperparameters of the algorithm, often with the objective of simplifying the algorithm's approximation of the data. For instance, for decision trees, this can be addressed by pruning the tree to delete some of the details that were learned from the training data. In neural networks, on the other hand, this can be addressed by adding regularization techniques that seek to reduce some of the neuron's influence on the overall result.

  Additionally, adding more data to the training set can also help the model avoid high variance, that is, increasing the dataset that's used for training the model.

- **Data mismatch**: This occurs when the training and validation sets do not follow the same distribution. This affects the model as although it generalizes based on the training data. This generalization does not describe the data that was found in the validation set. For instance, a model that's created to describe landscape photographs may suffer from a data mismatch if it is trained using high-definition images, while the actual images that will be used once the model has been built are unprofessional.

  Logically, the best way to avoid data mismatch is to make sure that the sets follow the same distribution. For example, you can do this by shuffling together the images from both sources (professional and unprofessional images) and then dividing them into the different sets.

  Nevertheless, in cases where there is not enough data that follows the same distribution of unseen data (data that will be used in the future), it is highly recommended to create the dev and test sets entirely out of that data and add the remaining data to the large training set. From the preceding example, the unprofessional images should be used to create the dev and test sets, adding the remaining ones to the training set, along with the professional images. This helps to train a model with a set that contains enough images to make a generalization, but it uses data with the same distribution as the unseen data to fine-tune the model.

  Finally, if the data from all sets comes from the same distribution, this condition actually refers to a problem of high variance and should be handled as such.

- **Overfitting to the dev set**: Lastly, similar to the variance condition, this occurs when the model is not generalizing but instead is fitting the dev set too well.

  It should be addressed using the same approaches that were explained for high variance.

In the next exercise, we will calculate the error rate of the model on the different sets of data, which can be used to perform error analysis.

EXERCISE 3.05: CALCULATING THE ERROR RATE ON DIFFERENT SETS OF DATA

In this exercise, we will calculate error rates for a model that has been trained using a decision tree. We will use the breast cancer dataset for this purpose. Follow these steps to complete this exercise:

1. Open a Jupyter Notebook to implement this exercise and import all the required elements to load and split the dataset. These will be used to train a model and evaluate its recall:

```
from sklearn.datasets import load_breast_cancer
import pandas as pd
from sklearn.model_selection import train_test_split
import numpy as np
from sklearn import tree
from sklearn.metrics import recall_score
```

2. For this exercise, the **breast cancer** dataset will be used. Use the following code to load the dataset and create the Pandas DataFrames containing the features and target matrices:

```
breast_cancer = load_breast_cancer()
X = pd.DataFrame(breast_cancer.data)
Y = pd.DataFrame(breast_cancer.target)
```

3. Split the dataset into training, validation, and testing sets:

```
X_new, X_test, Y_new, Y_test = train_test_split(X, Y, \
                        test_size = 0.1, random_state = 101)


test_size = X_test.shape[0] / X_new.shape[0]


X_train, X_dev, Y_train, Y_dev = train_test_split(X_new, Y_new, \
                        test_size = test_size, \
                        random_state = 101)
```

```
print(X_train.shape, Y_train.shape, X_dev.shape, \
      Y_dev.shape, X_test.shape, Y_test.shape)
```

The resulting shapes are as follows:

```
(455, 30) (455, 1) (57, 30) (57, 1) (57, 30) (57, 1)
```

4. Create a train/dev set that combines data from both the training and validation sets:

```
np.random.seed(101)

indices_train = np.random.randint(0, len(X_train), 25)
indices_dev = np.random.randint(0, len(X_dev), 25)

X_train_dev = pd.concat([X_train.iloc[indices_train,:], \
                         X_dev.iloc[indices_dev,:]])

Y_train_dev = pd.concat([Y_train.iloc[indices_train,:], \
                         Y_dev.iloc[indices_dev,:]])

print(X_train_dev.shape, Y_train_dev.shape)
```

First, a random seed is set to ensure the reproducibility of the results. Next, the NumPy **random.randint()** function is used to select random indices from the **X_train** set. To do that, 28 random integers are generated in a range between 0 and the total length of **X_train**. The same process is used to generate the random indices of the dev set. Finally, a new variable is created to store the selected values of **X_train** and **X_dev**, as well as a variable to store the corresponding values from **Y_train** and **Y_dev**.

The variables that have been created contain 25 instances/labels from the train set and 25 instances/labels from the dev set.

The resulting shapes of the sets are as follows:

```
(50, 30) (50, 1)
```

5. Train a decision tree on the train set, as follows:

```
model = tree.DecisionTreeClassifier(random_state = 101)
model = model.fit(X_train, Y_train)
```

6. Use the **predict** method to generate the predictions for all of your sets (train, train/dev, dev, and test). Next, considering that the objective of the study is to maximize the model's ability to predict all malignant cases, calculate the recall scores for all predictions. Store all of the scores in a variable named **scores**:

```
sets = ["Training", "Train/dev", "Validation", "Testing"]
X_sets = [X_train, X_train_dev, X_dev, X_test]
Y_sets = [Y_train, Y_train_dev, Y_dev, Y_test]

scores = {}
for i in range(0, len(X_sets)):
    pred = model.predict(X_sets[i])
    score = recall_score(Y_sets[i], pred)
    scores[sets[i]] = score

print(scores)
```

The error rates for all of the sets of data are as follows:

```
{'Training': 1.0, 'Train/dev': 0.9705882352941176, 'Validation':
0.9333333333333333, 'Testing': 0.9714285714285714}
```

From the preceding values, the following table containing the error rates can be created:

Sets	Error Rate
Bayes error	0
Training set	0
Train/dev set	0.0295
Validation set	0.0667
Testing set	0.0286

Figure 3.12: Error rates for all sets of data

Here, the Bayes error was assumed as **0**, considering that the classification between a malignant and a benign mass is done by taking a biopsy of the mass.

From the preceding table, it can be concluded that the model performs exceptionally well for the purpose of the study, considering that all error rates are close to 0, which is the lowest possible error.

The highest difference in error rates is found between the train/dev set and the dev set, which refers to data mismatch. However, taking into account that all the datasets come from the same distribution, this condition is considered a high variance issue, where adding more data to the training set should help reduce the error rate.

> **NOTE**
>
> To access the source code for this specific section, please refer to https://packt.live/3e4Toer.
>
> You can also run this example online at https://packt.live/2UJzDkW. You must execute the entire Notebook in order to get the desired result.

You have successfully calculated the error rate of all the subsets of data. In the next activity, we will perform an error analysis to define the steps to be taken to improve the performance of a model that was created to recognize handwritten digits.

ACTIVITY 3.03: PERFORMING ERROR ANALYSIS ON A MODEL TRAINED TO RECOGNIZE HANDWRITTEN DIGITS

Based on the different metrics that you have provided to your team to measure the performance of the model, they have selected accuracy as the ideal metric. Considering this, your team has asked you to perform an error analysis to determine how the model could be improved. In this activity, you will perform an error analysis by comparing the error rate of the different sets in terms of the accuracy of the model. Follow these steps to achieve this:

1. Import the required elements to load and split a dataset. We will do this to train the model and measure its accuracy.

2. Load the **digits** toy dataset from scikit-learn and create Pandas DataFrames containing the features and target matrices.

3. Split the data into training, validation, and testing sets. Use 0.1 as the size of the test set, and an equivalent number to build a validation set of the same shape.

4. Create a train/dev set for both the features and target values that contains 90 instances/labels of the train set and 90 instances/labels of the dev set.

5. Train a decision tree on that training set data.

6. Calculate the error rate for all sets of data in terms of the accuracy of the model and determine which condition is affecting the performance of the model.

By completing this activity, you should obtain the following error rates:

Sets	Error Rate
Bayes error	0
Training set	0
Train/dev set	0.0556
Validation set	0.1167
Testing set	0.1167

Figure 3.13: Expected error rates

> **NOTE**
>
> The solution for this activity can be found on page 233.

SUMMARY

This chapter explained the different tasks that can be solved through supervised learning algorithms: classification and regression. Although both of these tasks' goal is to approximate a function that maps a set of features to an output, classification tasks have a discrete number of outputs, while regression tasks can have infinite continuous values as outputs.

When developing machine learning models to solve supervised learning problems, one of the main goals is for the model to be capable of generalizing so that it will be applicable to future unseen data, instead of just learning a set of instances very well but performing poorly on new data. Accordingly, a methodology for validation and testing was explained in this chapter, which involved splitting the data into three sets: a training set, a dev set, and a test set. This approach eliminates the risk of bias.

After this, we covered how to evaluate the performance of a model for both classification and regression problems. Finally, we covered how to analyze the performance of a model and perform error analysis on each of the sets to detect the condition affecting the model's performance.

In the next chapter, we will focus on applying different algorithms to a real-life dataset, with the underlying objective of applying the steps we learned about here to choose the best performing algorithm for the case study.

SUPERVISED LEARNING ALGORITHMS: PREDICTING ANNUAL INCOME

OVERVIEW

In this chapter, we will take a look at three different supervised learning algorithms used for classification. We will also solve a supervised learning classification problem using these algorithms and perform error analysis by comparing the results of the three different algorithms.

By the end of this chapter, you will be able to identify the algorithm with the best performance.

INTRODUCTION

In the previous chapter, we covered the key steps involved in working with a supervised learning data problem. Those steps aim to create high-performing algorithms, as explained in the previous chapter.

This chapter focuses on applying different algorithms to a real-life dataset, with the underlying objective of applying the steps that we learned previously to choose the best-performing algorithm for the case study. Considering this, you will pre-process and analyze a dataset, and then create three models using different algorithms. These models will be compared to one another in order to measure their performance.

The Census Income dataset that we'll be using contains demographical and financial information, which can be used to try and predict the level of income of an individual. By creating a model capable of predicting this outcome for new observations, it will be possible to determine whether a person can be pre-approved to receive a loan.

EXPLORING THE DATASET

Real-life applications are crucial for cementing knowledge. Therefore, this chapter consists of a real-life case study involving a classification task, where the key steps that you learned about in the previous chapter will be applied in order to select the best performing model.

To accomplish this, the Census Income dataset will be used, which is available at the UC Irvine Machine Learning Repository.

> **NOTE**
>
> The dataset that will be used in the following section, as well as in this chapter's activities, can be found in this book's GitHub repository at https://packt.live/2xUGShx.
>
> Citation: Dua, D. and Graff, C. (2019). UCI Machine Learning Repository [http://archive.ics.uci.edu/ml]. Irvine, CA: University of California, School of Information and Computer Science.

You can download the dataset from this book's GitHub repository. Alternatively, to download the dataset from the original source, follow these steps:

1. Visit the following link: http://archive.ics.uci.edu/ml/datasets/Census+Income.

2. First, click the **Data Folder** link.

3. For this chapter, the data available under **adult.data** will be used. Once you click this link, the download will be triggered. Save it as a **.csv** file.

> **NOTE**
>
> Open the file and add header names over each column to make pre-processing easier. For instance, the first column should have the header **Age**, as per the features available in the dataset. These can be seen in the preceding link, under **Attribute Information**.

UNDERSTANDING THE DATASET

To build a model that fits the data accurately, it is important to understand the different details of the dataset, as mentioned in previous chapters.

First, the data that's available is revised to understand the size of the dataset and the type of supervised learning task to be developed: classification or regression. Next, the purpose of the study should be clearly defined, even if it is obvious. For supervised learning, the purpose is closely linked to the class labels. Finally, each feature is analyzed so that we can be aware of their types for pre-processing purposes.

The Census Income dataset is a collection of demographical data on adults, which is an extract from the 1994 Census Database from the United States. For this chapter, only the data available under the **adult.data** link will be used. The dataset consists of 32,561 instances, 14 features, and 1 binary class label. Considering that the class label is discrete, our task is to achieve the classification of the different observations.

> **NOTE**
>
> The following exploration of the dataset does not require coding of any sort, but rather a simple evaluation by opening the dataset in Excel or a similar program.

Through a quick evaluation of the data, it is possible to observe that some features present missing values in the form of a question mark. This is common when dealing with datasets that are available online and should be handled by replacing the symbol with an empty value (not a space). Other common forms of missing values are the **NULL** value and a dash.

To edit missing value symbols in Excel, use the **Replace** functionality, as follows:

- **Find what**: Input the symbol that is being used to signify a missing value (for example, **?**).

- **Replace with**: Leave it blank (do not enter a space).

This way, once we import the dataset into the code, NumPy will be able to find the missing values so that it can handle them.

The prediction task for this dataset involves determining whether a person earns over 50K dollars a year. According to this, the two possible outcome labels are **>50K** (greater than 50K) or **<=50K** (less than, or equal to 50K).

A brief explanation of each of the features in the dataset is shown in the following table:

Feature	Type	Note	Relevant
age	Quantitative (continuous)	The age of the individual	Yes
workclass	Qualitative (nominal)	The type of employment of the individual	Yes
fnlwgt	Quantitative (continuous)	The number of people the census takers believe the individual represents	No; the values were subjective to the census taker
education	Qualitative (ordinal)	The highest education level achieved, by the individual	No; the education-num feature represents the same information but is preferred because it is presented in numerical form
education-num	Quantitative (discrete)	The highest education level achieved in numerical form	Yes
marital-status	Qualitative (nominal)	The marital status of the individual	Yes
occupation	Qualitative (nominal)	The current occupation of the individual	Yes
relationship	Qualitative (nominal)	A relationship value that represents the individual	No; this feature is ignored since its purpose is not clear
race	Qualitative (nominal)	The race of the individual	Although (in some cases) this feature may be relevant, for ethical reasons, it will be excluded from the study*
sex	Qualitative (nominal)	The gender of the individual	Although (in some cases) this feature may be relevant, for ethical reasons, it will be excluded from the study*
capital-gain	Quantitative (continuous)	All of the individual's recorded capital gains	Yes
capital-loss	Quantitative (continuous)	All of the individual's recorded capital loss	Yes
hours-per-week	Quantitative (continuous)	The number of hours that the individual works per week	Yes
native-country	Qualitative (nominal)	The native country of the individual	Yes

Figure 4.1: Dataset feature analysis

> **NOTE**
>
> *Publisher's Note: Gender and race would have impacted the earning potential of an individual at the date this study was conducted. However, for the purpose of this chapter, we have decided to exclude these categories from our exercises and activities.
>
> We recognize that due to biases and discriminatory practices, it is impossible to separate issues such as gender, race, and educational and vocational opportunities. The removal of certain features from our dataset in the pre-processing stage of these exercises is not intended to ignore the issues, nor the valuable work undertaken by organizations and individuals working in the civil rights sphere.
>
> We strongly recommend that you consider the sociopolitical impacts of data and the way it is used, and also consider how past prejudices can be perpetuated by using historical data to introduce bias into new algorithms.

From the preceding table, it is possible to conclude the following:

- Five features are not relevant to the study: **fnlwgt**, **education**, **relationship**, **race**, and **sex**. These features must be deleted from the dataset before we proceed with pre-processing and training the model.

- Out of the remaining features, four are presented as qualitative values. Considering that many algorithms do not take qualitative features into account, the values should be represented in numerical form.

Using the concepts that we learned about in the previous chapters, the preceding statements, as well as the pre-processing process for handling outliers and missing values, can be taken care of. The following steps explain the logic of this process:

1. You need to import the dataset and drop the features that are irrelevant to the study.

2. You should check for missing values. Considering the feature with the most missing values (**occupation**, with 1,843 missing values), there will be no need to delete or replace the missing values as they represent only 5% or less of the entire dataset.

3. You must convert the qualitative values into their numeric representations.

4. You should check for outliers. Upon using three standard deviations to detect outliers, the feature with the maximum number of outliers is **capital-loss**, which contains 1,470 outliers. Again, the outliers represent less than 5% of the entire dataset, meaning they can be left untouched without impacting the result of the model.

The preceding process will convert the original dataset into a new dataset with 32,561 instances (since no instances were deleted), but with 9 features and a class label. All values should be in their numerical forms. Save the pre-processed dataset into a file using pandas' **to_csv** function, as per the following code snippet:

```
preprocessed_data.to_csv("census_income_dataset_preprocessed.csv")
```

The preceding code snippet takes the pre-processed data stored in a Pandas DataFrame and saves it into a CSV file.

> **NOTE**
>
> Make sure that you perform the preceding pre-processing steps, as this is the dataset that will be used for training the models in the different activities of this chapter.
>
> To review these steps, visit the GitHub repository of this book, under the folder named **Chapter04**, in the file named **Census income dataset preprocessing**.

THE NAÏVE BAYES ALGORITHM

Naïve Bayes is a classification algorithm based on **Bayes' theorem** that *naïvely* assumes independence between features and assigns the same weight (degree of importance) to all features. This means that the algorithm assumes that no single feature correlates to or affects another. For example, although weight and height are somehow correlated when predicting a person's age, the algorithm assumes that each feature is independent. Additionally, the algorithm considers all features equally important. For instance, even though an education degree may influence the earnings of a person to a greater degree than the number of children the person has, the algorithm still considers both features equally important.

> **NOTE**
>
> Bayes' theorem is a mathematical formula that calculates conditional probabilities. To learn more about this theorem, visit the following URL: https://plato.stanford.edu/entries/bayes-theorem/.

Although real-life datasets contain features that are not equally important, nor independent, this algorithm is popular among scientists as it performs surprisingly well on large datasets. Also, due to the simplistic approach of the algorithm, it runs quickly, thus allowing it to be applied to problems that require predictions in real-time. Moreover, it is frequently used for text classification as it commonly outperforms more complex algorithms.

HOW DOES THE NAÏVE BAYES ALGORITHM WORK?

The algorithm converts the input data into a summary of occurrences of each class label against each feature, which is then used to calculate the likelihood of one event (a class label), given a combination of features. Finally, this likelihood is normalized against the likelihood of the other class labels. The result is the probability of an instance belonging to each class label. The sum of the probabilities must be one, and the class label with a higher probability is the one that the algorithm chooses as the prediction.

Let's take, for example, the data presented in the following tables:

A		
Weather	**Temperature**	**Outcome**
Sunny	Hot	Yes
Sunny	Cool	Yes
Rainy	Cold	No
Sunny	Hot	No
Mild	Cool	Yes
Mild	Cool	Yes
Sunny	Hot	Yes
Rainy	Cool	No
Rainy	Cold	Yes
Sunny	Hot	Yes

B		
Weather	**Temperature**	**Outcome**
Sunny	4	1
Rainy	1	2
Mild	2	0

Temprature	**Yes**	**No**
Hot	3	1
Cool	3	1
Cold	1	1

Overall	**Yes**	**No**
	7	3

Figure 4.2: Table A - Input data and Table B - Occurrence count

Table A represents the data that is fed to the algorithm to build the model. Table B refer to the occurrence count that the algorithm uses implicitly to calculate the probabilities.

To calculate the likelihood of an event occurring when given a set of features, the algorithm multiplies the probability of the event occurring, given each individual feature, by the probability of the occurrence of the event, independent of the rest of the features, as follows:

```
Likelihood [A₁|E] = P[A₁|E₁] * P[A₁|E₂] * … * P[A₁|Eₙ] * P[A₁]
```

Here, A_1 refers to an event (one of the class labels) and E represents the set of features, where E_1 is the first feature and E_n is the last feature in the dataset.

> **NOTE**
>
> The multiplication of these probabilities can only be made by assuming independence between features.

The preceding equation is calculated for all possible outcomes (all class labels), and then the normalized probability of each outcome is calculated as follows:

$$P[A_1|E] = \frac{likelihood[A_1|E]}{likelihood[A_1|E] + likelihood[A_2|E] + \cdots + likelihood[A_n|E]}$$

Figure 4.3: Formula to calculate normalized probability

For the example in *Figure 4.2*, given a new instance with weather equal to *sunny* and temperature equal to *cool*, the calculation of probabilities is as follows:

$$Likelihood[yes|sunny, cool] = \frac{4}{7} * \frac{3}{7} * \frac{7}{10} = 0.17$$

$$Likelihood[no|sunny, cool] = \frac{1}{3} * \frac{1}{3} * \frac{3}{10} = 0.03$$

$$P[yes|sunny, cool] = \frac{0.17}{0.17 + 0.03} = 0.85 \approx 85\%$$

$$P[no|sunny, cool] = \frac{0.03}{0.17 + 0.03} = 0.15 \approx 15\%$$

Figure 4.4: Calculation of the likelihood and probabilities for the example dataset

By looking at the preceding equations, it is possible to conclude that the prediction should be *yes*.

It is important to mention that for continuous features, the summary of occurrences is done by creating ranges. For instance, for a feature of price, the algorithm may count the number of instances with prices below 100K, as well as the instances with prices above 100K.

Moreover, the algorithm may encounter some issues if one value of a feature is never associated with one of the outcomes. This is an issue mainly because the probability of the outcome given that feature will be zero, which influences the entire calculation. In the preceding example, for predicting the outcome of an instance with weather equal to *mild* and temperature equal to *cool*, the probability of *no*, given the set of features will be equal to zero, considering that the probability of *no*, given *mild* weather, computes to zero, since there are no occurrences of *mild* weather when the outcome is *no*.

To avoid this, the **Laplace estimator** technique should be used. Here, the fractions representing the probability of the occurrence of an event given a feature, $P[A|E_i]$, are modified by adding 1 to the numerator while also adding the number of possible values of that feature to the denominator.

For this example, to perform a prediction for a new instance with weather equal to *mild* and temperature equal to *cool* using the Laplace estimator, this would be done as follows:

$$Likelihood[yes|mild, cool] = \frac{3}{10} * \frac{4}{10} * \frac{7}{10} = 0.084$$

$$Likelihood[no|mild, cool] = \frac{1}{6} * \frac{2}{6} * \frac{3}{10} = 0.016$$

$$P[yes|mild, cool] = \frac{0.084}{0.084 + 0.016} = 0.84 \approx 84\%$$

$$P[no|mild, cool] = \frac{0.016}{0.084 + 0.016} = 0.16 \approx 16\%$$

Figure 4.5: Calculation of the likelihood and probability
using the Laplace estimator for the example dataset

Here, the fraction that calculates the occurrences of *yes*, given *mild* weather, goes from 2/7 to 3/10, as a result of the addition of 1 to the numerator and 3 (for *sunny*, *mild*, and *rainy*) to the denominator. The same goes for the other fractions that calculate the probability of the event, given a feature. Note that the fraction that calculates the probability of the event occurring independently of any feature is left unaltered.

Nevertheless, as you have learned so far, the scikit-learn library allows you to train models and then use them for predictions, without needing to hardcode the math.

EXERCISE 4.01: APPLYING THE NAÏVE BAYES ALGORITHM

Now, let's apply the Naïve Bayes algorithm to a Fertility dataset, which aims to determine whether the fertility level of an individual has been affected by their demographics, their environmental conditions, and their previous medical conditions. Follow these steps to complete this exercise:

> **NOTE**
>
> For the exercises and activities within this chapter, you will need to have Python 3.7, NumPy, Jupyter, Pandas, and scikit-learn installed on your system.

1. Download the Fertility dataset from http://archive.ics.uci.edu/ml/datasets/Fertility. Go to the link and click on **Data Folder**. Click on **fertility_Diagnosis. txt**, which will trigger the download. Save it as a **.csv** file.

> **NOTE**
>
> The dataset is also available in this book's GitHub repository at https://packt.live/39SsSSN.
>
> It was downloaded from the UC Irvine Machine Learning Repository: David Gil, Jose Luis Girela, Joaquin De Juan, M. Jose Gomez-Torres, and Magnus Johnsson. *Predicting seminal quality with artificial intelligence methods*. Expert Systems with Applications.

2. Open a Jupyter Notebook to implement this exercise. Import pandas, as well as the **GaussianNB** class from scikit-learn's **naive_bayes** module:

```
import pandas as pd
from sklearn.naive_bayes import GaussianNB
```

3. Read the **.csv** file that you downloaded in the first step. Make sure that you add the **header** argument equal to **None** to the **read_csv** function, considering that the dataset does not contain a header row:

```
data = pd.read_csv("fertility_Diagnosis.csv", header=None)
```

4. Split the data into **X** and **Y**, considering that the class label is found under the column with an index equal to 9. Use the following code to do so:

```
X = data.iloc[:,:9]
Y = data.iloc[:,9]
```

5. Instantiate the **GaussianNB** class that we imported previously. Next, use the **fit** method to train the model using **X** and **Y**:

```
model = GaussianNB()
model.fit(X, Y)
```

The output from running this script is as follows:

```
GaussianNB(priors=None, var_smoothing=1e-09)
```

This states that the instantiation of the class was successful. The information inside the parentheses represents the values used for the arguments that the class accepts, which are the hyperparameters.

For instance, for the **GaussianNB** class, it is possible to set the prior probabilities to consider for each class label and a smoothing argument that stabilizes variance. Nonetheless, the model was initialized without setting any arguments, which means that it will use the default values for each argument, which is **None** for the case of **priors** and **1e-09** for the smoothing hyperparameter.

6. Finally, perform a prediction using the model that you trained before, for a new instance with the following values for each feature: **−0.33, 0.69, 0, 1, 1, 0, 0.8, 0, 0.88**. Use the following code to do so:

```
pred = model.predict([[-0.33,0.69,0,1,1,0,0.8,0,0.88]])
print(pred)
```

Note that we feed the values inside of double square brackets, considering that the **predict** function takes in the values for prediction as an array of arrays, where the first set of arrays corresponds to the list of new instances to predict and the second array refers to the list of features for each instance.

The output from the preceding code snippet is as follows:

```
['N']
```

The predicted class for that subject is equal to **N**, which means that the fertility of the subject has not been affected.

> **NOTE**
>
> To access the source code for this specific section, please refer to https://packt.live/2Y2wW0c.
>
> You can also run this example online at https://packt.live/3e40LTt.
> You must execute the entire Notebook in order to get the desired result.

You have successfully trained a Naïve Bayes model and performed prediction on a new observation.

ACTIVITY 4.01: TRAINING A NAÏVE BAYES MODEL FOR OUR CENSUS INCOME DATASET

To test different classification algorithms on a real-life dataset, consider the following scenario: you work for a bank, and they have decided to implement a model that is able to predict a person's annual income and use that information to decide whether to approve a loan. You are given a dataset with 32,561 suitable observations, which you have already pre-processed. Your job is to train three different models on the dataset and determine which one best suits the case study. The first model to be built is a Gaussian Naïve Bayes model. Use the following steps to complete this activity:

1. In a Jupyter Notebook, import all the required elements to load and split the dataset, as well as to train a Naïve Bayes algorithm.

2. Load the pre-processed Census Income dataset. Next, separate the features from the target by creating two variables, **X** and **Y**.

> **NOTE**
>
> The pre-processed Census Income dataset can be found in this book's GitHub repository at https://packt.live/2JMhsFB. It consists of the transformed Census Income dataset that was pre-processed at the beginning of this chapter.

3. Divide the dataset into training, validation, and testing sets, using a split ratio of 10%.

> **NOTE**
>
> When all three sets are created from the same dataset, it is not required to create an additional train/dev set to measure data mismatch. Moreover, note that it is OK to try a different split ratio, considering that the percentages explained in the previous chapter are not set in stone. Even though they tend to work well, it is important that you embrace experimentation at different levels when building machine learning models.

4. Use the **fit** method to train a Naïve Bayes model on the training sets (**X_train** and **Y_train**).

5. Finally, perform a prediction using the model that you trained previously, for a new instance with the following values for each feature: **39**, **6**, **13**, **4**, 0, **2174**, 0, **40**, **38**.

   The prediction for the individual should be equal to zero, meaning that the individual most likely has an income less than or equal to 50K.

> **NOTE**
>
> Use the same Jupyter Notebook for all the activities within this chapter so that you can perform a comparison of different models on the same dataset.
>
> The solution for this activity can be found on page 236.

THE DECISION TREE ALGORITHM

The **decision tree algorithm** performs classification based on a sequence that resembles a tree-like structure. It works by dividing the dataset into small subsets that serve as guides to develop the decision tree nodes. The nodes can be either decision nodes or leaf nodes, where the former represent a question or decision, and the latter represent the decisions made or the final outcome.

HOW DOES THE DECISION TREE ALGORITHM WORK?

Considering what we just mentioned, decision trees continually split the dataset according to the parameters defined in the decision nodes. Decision nodes have branches coming out of them, where each decision node can have two or more branches. The branches represent the different possible answers that define the way in which the data is split.

For instance, consider the following table, which shows whether a person has a pending student loan based on their age, highest education, and current income:

Age	Highest Level of Education	Current Income	Target
25	Bachelor	0	Yes
32	Doctorate	120,000	Yes
48	Master	120,000	Yes
57	Master	150,000	No
29	College	50,000	No
35	Doctorate	230,000	No
69	Master	120,000	Yes
57	Doctorate	250,000	No
51	Bachelor	90,000	No
30	Master	115,000	Yes

Figure 4.6: Dataset for student loans

One possible configuration for a decision tree built based on the preceding data is shown in the following diagram, where the light boxes represent the decision nodes, the arrows are the branches representing each answer to the decision node, and the dark boxes refer to the outcome for instances that follow the sequence:

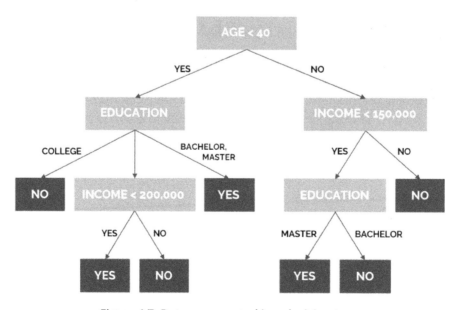

Figure 4.7: Data represented in a decision tree

To perform the prediction, once the decision tree has been built, the model takes each instance and follows the sequence that matches the instance's features until it reaches a leaf, that is, the outcome. According to this, the classification process starts at the root node (the one on top) and continues along the branch that describes the instance. This process continues until a leaf node is reached, which represents the prediction for that instance.

For instance, a person *over 40 years old* with an income *below $150,000* and an education level of *bachelor* is likely to not have a student loan; hence, the class label assigned to it would be *No*.

Decision trees can handle both quantitative and qualitative features, considering that continuous features will be handled in ranges. Additionally, leaf nodes can handle categorical or continuous class labels; for categorical class labels, a classification is made, while for continuous class labels, the task to be handled is regression.

EXERCISE 4.02: APPLYING THE DECISION TREE ALGORITHM

In this exercise, we will apply the decision tree algorithm to the Fertility Dataset, with the objective of determining whether the fertility level of an individual is affected by their demographics, their environmental conditions, and their previous medical conditions. Follow these steps to complete this exercise:

1. Open a Jupyter Notebook to implement this exercise and import **pandas**, as well as the **DecisionTreeClassifier** class from scikit-learn's **tree** module:

```
import pandas as pd
from sklearn.tree import DecisionTreeClassifier
```

2. Load the **fertility_Diagnosis** dataset that you downloaded in *Exercise 4.01*, *Applying the Naïve Bayes Algorithm*. Make sure that you add the **header** argument equal to **None** to the **read_csv** function, considering that the dataset does not contain a header row:

```
data = pd.read_csv("fertility_Diagnosis.csv", header=None)
```

3. Split the data into **X** and **Y**, considering that the class label is found under the column with the index equal to **9**. Use the following code:

```
X = data.iloc[:,:9]
Y = data.iloc[:,9]
```

4. Instantiate the **DecisionTreeClassifier** class. Next, use the **fit** function to train the model using **X** and **Y**:

```
model = DecisionTreeClassifier()
model.fit(X, Y)
```

Again, the output from running the preceding code snippet will appear. This output summarizes the conditions that define your model by printing the values that are used for every hyperparameter that the model uses, as follows:

```
DecisionTreeClassifier(ccp_alpha=0.0, class_weight=None,
                       criterion='gini', max_depth=None,
                       max_features=None, max_leaf_nodes=None,
                       min_impurity_decrease=0.0,
                       min_impurity_split=None,
                       min_samples_leaf=1, min_samples_split=2,
                       min_weight_fraction_leaf=0.0,
                       presort='deprecated',
                       random_state=None, splitter='best')
```

Since the model has been instantiated without setting any hyperparameters, the summary will show the default values that were used for each.

5. Finally, perform a prediction by using the model that you trained before, for the same instances that we used in *Exercise 4.01*, *Applying the Naïve Bayes Algorithm*: **−0.33, 0.69, 0, 1, 1, 0, 0.8, 0, 0.88**.

Use the following code to do so:

```
pred = model.predict([[-0.33,0.69,0,1,1,0,0.8,0,0.88]])
print(pred)
```

The output from the prediction is as follows:

```
['N']
```

Again, the model predicted that the fertility of the subject has not been affected.

> **NOTE**
>
> To access the source code for this specific section, please refer to https://packt.live/3hDlvns.
>
> You can also run this example online at https://packt.live/3fsVw07.
> You must execute the entire Notebook in order to get the desired result.

You have successfully trained a decision tree model and performed a prediction on new data.

ACTIVITY 4.02: TRAINING A DECISION TREE MODEL FOR OUR CENSUS INCOME DATASET

You continue to work on building a model that's able to predict a person's annual income. Using the pre-processed Census Income dataset, you have chosen to build a decision tree model:

1. Open the Jupyter Notebook that you used for the previous activity and import the decision tree algorithm from scikit-learn.

2. Train the model using the **fit** method on the **DecisionTreeClassifier** class from scikit-learn. To train the model, use the training set data from the previous activity (**X_train** and **Y_train**).

3. Finally, perform a prediction by using the model that you trained for a new instance with the following values for each feature: **39, 6, 13, 4, 0, 2174, 0, 40, 38**.

   The prediction for the individual should be equal to zero, meaning that the individual most likely has an income less than or equal to 50K.

   > **NOTE**
   >
   > The solution for this activity can be found on page 237.

THE SUPPORT VECTOR MACHINE ALGORITHM

The **Support Vector Machine** (**SVM**) algorithm is a classifier that finds the hyperplane that effectively separates the observations into their class labels. It starts by positioning each instance into a data space with *n* dimensions, where *n* represents the number of features. Next, it traces an imaginary line that clearly separates the instances belonging to a class label from the instances belonging to others.

A support vector refers to the coordinates of a given instance. According to this, the support vector machine is the boundary that effectively segregates the different support vectors in a data space.

For a two-dimensional data space, the hyperplane is a line that splits the data space into two sections, each one representing a class label.

HOW DOES THE SVM ALGORITHM WORK?

The following diagram shows a simple example of an SVM model. Both the triangles and circular data points represent the instances from the input dataset, where the shapes define the class label that each instance belongs to. The dashed line signifies the hyperplane that clearly segregates the data points, which is defined based on the data points' location in the data space. This line is used to classify unseen data, as represented by the square. This way, new instances that are located to the left of the line will be classified as triangles, while the ones to the right will be circles.

The larger the number of features, the more dimensions the data space will have, which will make visually representing the model impossible:

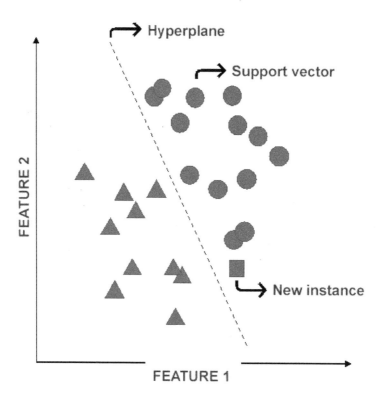

Figure 4.8: Graphical example of an SVM model

Although the algorithm seems to be quite simple, its complexity is evident in the algorithm's methodology for drawing the appropriate hyperplane. This is because the model generalizes to hundreds of observations with multiple features.

To choose the right hyperplane, the algorithm follows the following rules, wherein *Rule 1* is more important than *Rule 2*:

- **Rule 1**: The hyperplane must maximize the correct classification of instances. This basically means that the best line is the one that effectively separates data points belonging to different class labels while keeping those that belong to the same one together.

  For instance, in the following diagram, although both lines are able to separate most instances into their correct class labels, line A would be selected by the model as the one that segregates the classes better than line B, which fails to classify two data points:

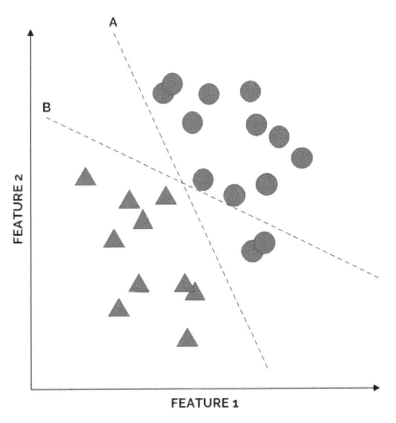

Figure 4.9: Sample of hyperplanes that explain Rule 1

- **Rule 2**: The hyperplane must maximize its distance to the nearest data point of either of the class labels, which is also known as the **margin**. This rule helps the model become more robust, which means that the model is able to generalize the input data so that it works efficiently on unseen data. This rule is especially important in preventing new instances from being mislabeled.

For example, by looking at the following diagram, it is possible to conclude that both hyperplanes comply with *Rule 1*. Nevertheless, line A is selected, since it maximizes its distance to the nearest data points for both classes in comparison to the distance of line B to its nearest data point:

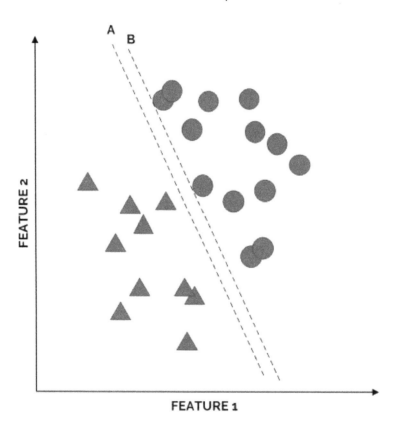

Figure 4.10: Sample of hyperplanes that explain Rule 2

By default, the SVM algorithm uses a linear function to split the data points of the input data. However, this configuration can be modified by changing the kernel type of the algorithm. For example, consider the following diagram:

> **NOTE**
>
> For scikit-learn's SVM algorithm, the kernel refers to the mathematical function to be used to split the data points, which can be linear, polynomial, or sigmoidal, among others. To learn more about the parameters for this algorithm, visit the following URL: https://scikit-learn.org/stable/modules/generated/sklearn.svm.SVC.html#sklearn.svm.SVC.

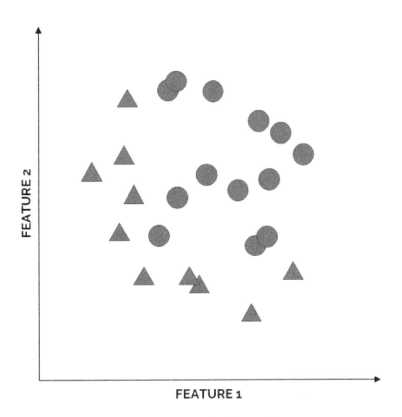

Figure 4.11: Sample observations

To segregate these observations, the model would have to draw a circle or another similar shape. The algorithm handles this by using kernels (mathematical functions) that can introduce additional features to the dataset in order to modify the distribution of data points into a form that allows a line to segregate them. There are several kernels available for this, and the selection of one should be done by trial and error so that you can find the one that best classifies the data that's available.

However, the default kernel for the SVM algorithm in scikit-learn is the **Radial Basis Function** (**RBF**) kernel. This is mainly because, based on several studies, this kernel has proved to work great for most data problems.

EXERCISE 4.03: APPLYING THE SVM ALGORITHM

In this exercise, we will apply the SVM algorithm to the Fertility dataset. The idea, which is the same as in previous exercises, is to determine whether the fertility level of an individual is affected by their demographics, their environmental conditions, and their previous medical conditions. Follow these steps to complete this exercise:

1. Open a Jupyter Notebook to implement this exercise. Import pandas as well as the **SVC** class from scikit-learn's **svm** module:

```
import pandas as pd
from sklearn.svm import SVC
```

2. Load the **fertility_Diagnosis** dataset that you downloaded in *Exercise 4.01, Applying the Naïve Bayes Algorithm*. Make sure to add the **header = None** argument to the **read_csv** function, considering that the dataset does not contain a header row:

```
data = pd.read_csv("fertility_Diagnosis.csv", header=None)
```

3. Split the data into **X** and **Y**, considering that the class label is found under the column with the index equal to **9**. Use the following code to do so:

```
X = data.iloc[:,:9]
Y = data.iloc[:,9]
```

4. Instantiate scikit-learn's **SVC** class and use the **fit** function to train the model using **X** and **Y**:

```
model = SVC()
model.fit(X, Y)
```

Again, the output from running this code represents the summary of the model, along with its default hyperparameters, as follows:

```
SVC(C=1.0, break_ties=False, cache_size=200,
    class_weight=None, coef0=0.0,
    decision_function_shape='ovr', degree=3,
    gamma='scale', kernel='rbf', max_iter=-1,
    probability=False, random_state=None, shrinking=True,
    tol=0.001, verbose=False)
```

5. Finally, perform a prediction using the model that you trained previously, for the same instances that we used in *Exercise 4.01, Applying the Naïve Bayes Algorithm*: $-0.33, 0.69, 0, 1, 1, 0, 0.8, 0, 0.88$.

Use the following code to do so:

```
pred = model.predict([[-0.33,0.69,0,1,1,0,0.8,0,0.88]])
print(pred)
```

The output is as follows:

```
['N']
```

Again, the model predicts the instance's class label as **N**, meaning that the fertility of the subject has not been affected.

> **NOTE**
>
> To access the source code for this specific section, please refer to https://packt.live/2YyEMNX.
>
> You can also run this example online at https://packt.live/2Y3nIR2.
> You must execute the entire Notebook in order to get the desired result.

You have successfully trained an SVM model and performed a prediction.

ACTIVITY 4.03: TRAINING AN SVM MODEL FOR OUR CENSUS INCOME DATASET

Continuing with your task of building a model that is capable of predicting a person's annual income, the final algorithm that you want to train is the Support Vector Machine. Follow these steps to implement this activity:

1. Open the Jupyter Notebook that you used for the previous activity and import the SVM algorithm from scikit-learn.

2. Train the model using the **fit** method on the **SVC** class from scikit-learn. To train the model, use the training set data from the previous activity (**X_train** and **Y_train**).

   > **NOTE**
   >
   > The process of training the SVC class using the **fit** method may take a while.

3. Finally, perform a prediction using the model that you trained previously, for a new instance with the following values for each feature: **39, 6, 13, 4, 0, 2174, 0, 40, 38.**

   The prediction for the individual should be equal to zero, that is, the individual most likely has an income less than or equal to 50K.

   > **NOTE**
   >
   > The solution for this activity can be found on page 238.

ERROR ANALYSIS

In the previous chapter, we explained the importance of error analysis. In this section, the different evaluation metrics will be calculated for all three models that were created in the previous activities so that we can compare them.

For learning purposes, we will compare the models using accuracy, precision, and recall metrics. This way, it will be possible to see that even though a model might be better in terms of one metric, it could be worse when measuring a different metric, which helps to emphasize the importance of choosing the right metric to measure your model according to the goal you wish to achieve.

ACCURACY, PRECISION, AND RECALL

As a quick reminder, in order to measure performance and perform error analysis, it is required that you use the **predict** method for the different sets of data (training, validation, and testing). The following code snippets present a clean way of measuring all three metrics on our three sets at once:

> **NOTE**
>
> The following steps are to be performed after solving the activities of this chapter. This is mainly because the steps in this section correspond to a continuation of this chapter's activities.

1. First, the three metrics to be used are imported:

```
from sklearn.metrics import accuracy_score, \
precision_score, recall_score
```

2. Next, we create two lists containing the different sets of data that will be used inside a **for** loop to perform the performance calculation on all sets of data for all models:

```
X_sets = [X_train, X_dev, X_test]
Y_sets = [Y_train, Y_dev, Y_test]
```

3. A dictionary will be created, which will hold the value of each evaluation metric for each set of data for each model:

```
metrics = {"NB":{"Acc":[],"Pre":[],"Rec":[]},
           "DT":{"Acc":[],"Pre":[],"Rec":[]},
           "SVM":{"Acc":[],"Pre":[],"Rec":[]}}
```

4. A **for** loop is used to go through the different sets of data:

```
for i in range(0,len(X_sets)):
    pred_NB = model_NB.predict(X_sets[i])
    metrics["NB"]["Acc"].append(accuracy_score(Y_sets[i], \
                        pred_NB))
    metrics["NB"]["Pre"].append(precision_score(Y_sets[i], \
                        pred_NB))
    metrics["NB"]["Rec"].append(recall_score(Y_sets[i], \
                        pred_NB))
```

```
    pred_tree = model_tree.predict(X_sets[i])
    metrics["DT"]["Acc"].append(accuracy_score(Y_sets[i], \
                            pred_tree))
    metrics["DT"]["Pre"].append(precision_score(Y_sets[i], \
                            pred_tree))
    metrics["DT"]["Rec"].append(recall_score(Y_sets[i], \
                            pred_tree))


    pred_svm = model_svm.predict(X_sets[i])
    metrics["SVM"]["Acc"].append(accuracy_score(Y_sets[i], \
                            pred_svm))
    metrics["SVM"]["Pre"].append(precision_score(Y_sets[i], \
                            pred_svm))
    metrics["SVM"]["Rec"].append(recall_score(Y_sets[i], \
                            pred_svm))
```

5. Print the metrics, as follows:

```
print(metrics)
```

The output is as follows:

```
{'NB': {'Acc': [0.7970975544208546, 0.7902978200798281, 0.8084126496776174],
  'Pre': [0.6683725690890481, 0.6816901408450704, 0.6873239436619718],
  'Rec': [0.3123405612244898, 0.29802955665024633, 0.32232496697490093]},
 'DT': {'Acc': [0.9723960532882866, 0.8114829597789377, 0.8234571691740866],
  'Pre': [0.9827856025039123, 0.6316489361702128, 0.6226415094339622],
  'Rec': [0.9011479591836735, 0.5849753694581281, 0.6103038309114928]},
 'SVM': {'Acc': [0.8024724536414942, 0.7958243782622045, 0.8099478047282775],
  'Pre': [0.7411210954214805, 0.7474747474747475, 0.7429577464788732],
  'Rec': [0.27614795918367346, 0.2733990147783251, 0.27873183619550856]}}
```

Figure 4.12: Printing the metrics

Inside the **for** loop, there are three blocks of code, one for each model we created in the previous activities. Each block of code performs the following actions.

First, a prediction is made. The prediction is achieved by calling the **predict** method on the model and inputting a set of data. As this operation occurs inside a **for** loop, the prediction will occur for all sets of data.

Next, the calculation of all three metrics is done by comparing the ground truth data with the prediction that we calculated previously. The calculation is appended to the dictionary that was created previously.

From the preceding snippets, the following results are obtained:

		Naïve Bayes	Decision Tree	SVM
Accuracy	Training sets	0.7971	0.9724	0.8025
	Validation sets	0.7902	0.8115	0.7958
	Testing sets	0.8084	0.8235	0.8099
Precision	Training sets	0.6684	0.9828	0.7411
	Validation sets	0.6817	0.6316	0.7475
	Testing sets	0.6873	0.6226	0.7429
Recall	Training sets	0.3123	0.9011	0.2761
	Validation sets	0.2980	0.5849	0.2734
	Testing sets	0.3223	0.6103	0.2787

Figure 4.13: Performance results of all three models

> **NOTE**
>
> Review the code to arrive at these results, which can be found in this book's GitHub repository, under the folder named **Chapter04**, by opening the file named **Error analysis**.

Initially, the following inferences, in relation to selecting the best-fitted model, as well as with regard to the conditions that each model suffers from, will be done while considering only the values from the accuracy metric, assuming a Bayes error of close to 0 (meaning that the model could reach a maximum success rate of close to 1):

- Upon comparing the three accuracy scores of the Naïve Bayes and the SVM models, it is possible to conclude that the models behave almost the same way for all three sets of data. This basically means that the models are generalizing the data from the training set, which allows them to perform well on unseen data. Nevertheless, the overall performance of the models is around 0.8, which is far from the maximum success rate. This means that the models may be suffering from high bias.

- Moreover, the performance of the decision tree model, in terms of the accuracy of the training set, is closer to the maximum success rate. However, the model is suffering from a case of overfitting, considering that the accuracy level of the model on the validation set is much lower than its performance on the training set. According to this, it would be possible to address the overfitting issue by adding more data to the training set or by fine-tuning the hyperparameters of the model, which would help to bring up the accuracy level of the validation and testing sets. Pruning the tree can help an overfitted model.

Considering this, the researcher now has the required information to select a model and work on improving the results to achieve the maximum possible performance of the model.

Next, for learning purposes, let's compare the results of all the metrics for the decision tree model. Although the values for all three metrics prove the existence of overfitting, it is possible to observe that the degree of overfitting is much larger for the precision and recall metrics. Also, it is possible to conclude that the performance of the model on the training set measured by the recall metric is much lower, which means that the model is not as good at classifying positive labels. This means that if the purpose of the case study was to maximize the number of positive classifications, regardless of the classification of negative labels, the model would also need to improve its performance on the training set.

> **NOTE**
>
> The preceding comparison is done to show that the performance of the same model can vary if measured with a different metric. According to this, it is crucial to choose the metric of relevance for the case study.

Using the knowledge that you have gained from previous chapters, feel free to keep exploring the results shown in the preceding table.

SUMMARY

Using the knowledge from previous chapters, we started this chapter by performing an analysis of the Census Income dataset, with the objective of understanding the data that's available and making decisions about the pre-processing process. Three supervised learning classification algorithms—the Naïve Bayes algorithm, the Decision Tree algorithm, and the SVM algorithm—were explained, and were applied to the previously pre-processed dataset to create models that generalized to the training data. Finally, we compared the performance of the three models on the Census Income dataset by calculating the accuracy, precision, and recall on the different sets of data (training, validation, and testing).

In the next chapter, we will look at **Artificial Neural Networks** (**ANNs**), their different types, and their advantages and disadvantages. We will also use an ANN to solve the same data problem that was discussed in this chapter, as well as to compare its performance with that of the other supervised learning algorithms.

5

SUPERVISED LEARNING – KEY STEPS

OVERVIEW

In this chapter, we will dive deep into the concept of neural networks and describe the processes of forward and backpropagation. We will solve a supervised learning classification problem using a neural network and analyze the results of the neural network by performing error analysis.

By the end of this chapter, you will be able to train a network to solve a classification problem and fine-tune some of the hyperparameters of the network to improve its performance.

INTRODUCTION

In the preceding chapter, we explored three machine learning algorithms to solve supervised learning tasks, either for classification or regression. In this chapter, we will explore one of the most popular machine learning algorithms nowadays, artificial neural networks, which belong to a subgroup of machine learning called deep learning.

Artificial neural networks (**ANNs**), also known as **Multilayer Perceptrons** (**MLPs**), have become increasingly popular mostly because they present a complex algorithm that can approach almost any challenging data problem. Even though the theory was developed decades back, during the 1940s, such networks are becoming more popular now, thanks to all the improvements in technology that allow for the gathering of large amounts of data, as well as the developments in computer infrastructure that allow the training of complex algorithms with large amounts of data.

Due to this, the following chapter will focus on introducing ANNs, their different types, and the advantages and disadvantages that they present. Additionally, an ANN will be used to predict the income of an individual based on demographic and financial information from the individual, as per the previous chapter, in order to present the differences in the performance of ANNs in comparison to the other supervised learning algorithms.

ARTIFICIAL NEURAL NETWORKS

Although there are several machine learning algorithms available to solve data problems, as we have already stated, ANNs have become increasingly popular among data scientists, on account of their ability to find patterns in large and complex datasets that cannot be interpreted by humans.

The **neural** part of the name refers to the resemblance of the architecture of the model to the anatomy of the human brain. This part is meant to replicate a human being's ability to learn from historical data by transferring bits of data from neuron to neuron until an outcome is reached.

In the following diagram, a human neuron is displayed, where A represents the **dendrites** that receive input information from other neurons, B refers to the **nucleus** of the neuron that processes the information, and C represents the **axon** that oversees the process of passing the processed information to the next neuron:

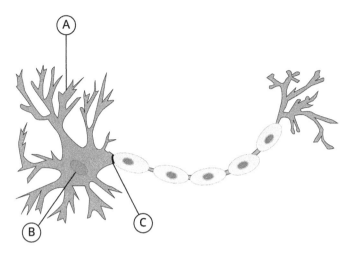

Figure 5.1: Visual representation of a human neuron

Moreover, the **artificial** part refers to the actual learning process of the model, where the main objective is to minimize the error in the model. This is an artificial learning process, considering that there is no real evidence regarding how human neurons process the information that they receive, and hence the model relies on mathematical functions that map an input to a desired output.

HOW DO ANNS WORK?

Before we dive into the process that is followed by an ANN, let's start by looking at its main components:

- **Input layer**: This layer is also known as **X**, as it contains all the data from the dataset (each instance with its features).

- **Hidden layers**: This layer is in charge of processing the input data in order to find patterns that are useful for making a prediction. The ANN can have as many hidden layers as desired, each with as many neurons (units) as required. The first layers are in charge of the simpler patterns, while the layers at the end search for the more complex ones.

  The hidden layers use a set of variables that represent weights and biases in order to help train the network. The values for the weights and biases are used as the variables that change in each iteration to approximate the prediction to the ground truth. This will be explained later.

- **Output layer**: Also known as `Y_hat`, this layer is the prediction made by the model, based on the data received from the hidden layers. This prediction is presented in the form of a probability, where the class label with a higher probability is the one selected as the prediction.

The following diagram illustrates the architecture of the preceding three layers, where the circles under 1 denote the neurons in the input layer, the ones under 2 represent the neurons of 2 hidden layers (each layer represented by a column of circles), and finally, the circles under 3 are the neurons of the output layer:

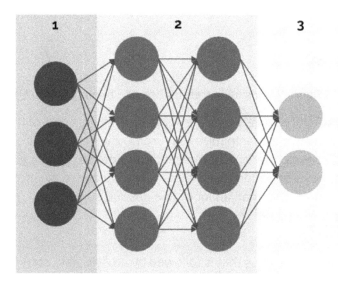

Figure 5.2: Basic architecture of an ANN

As an analogy, consider a manufacturing process for building car parts. Here, the input layer consists of the raw materials, which, in this case, may be aluminum. The initial steps of the process involve polishing and cleaning the material, which can be seen as the first couple of hidden layers. Next, the material is bent to achieve the shape of the car part, which is handled by the deeper hidden layers. Finally, the part is delivered to the client, which can be considered to be the output layer.

Considering these steps, the main objective of the manufacturing process is to achieve a final part that highly resembles the part that the process aimed to build, meaning that the output, `Y_hat`, should maximize its similarity to **Y** (the ground truth) for a model to be considered a good fit to the data.

The actual methodology to train an ANN is an iterative process comprised of the following steps: forward propagation, calculation of the cost function, backpropagation, and weights and biases updates. Once the weights and biases are updated, the process starts again until the number of iterations is met.

Let's explore each of the steps of the iteration process in detail.

FORWARD PROPAGATION

The input layer feeds the initial information to the ANN. The processing of the data is done by propagating data bits through the depth (number of hidden layers) and width (number of units in each layer) of the network. The information is processed by each neuron in each layer using a linear function, coupled with an activation function that aims to break the linearity, as follows:

$$Z_1 = W_1 * X + b_1$$

$$A_1 = \sigma(Z_1)$$

Figure 5.3: The linear and activation functions used by an ANN

Here, W_1 and b_1 are a matrix and a vector containing the weights and biases, respectively, and serve as the variables that can be updated through the iterations to train the model. Z_1 is the linear function for a given neuron, and A_1 is the outcome from the unit after applying an activation function (represented by the sigma symbol) to the linear one.

The preceding two formulas are calculated for each neuron in each layer, where the value of X for the hidden layers (other than the input layer) is replaced by the output of the previous layer (A_n), as follows:

$$Z_2 = W_2 * A_1 + b_2$$

$$A_2 = \sigma(Z_2)$$

Figure 5.4: The values calculated for the second layer of the ANN

Finally, the output from the last hidden layer is fed to the output layer, where the linear function is once again calculated, along with an activation function. The outcome from this layer, after some processing as required, is the one that will be compared against the ground truth in order to evaluate the performance of the algorithm before moving on to the next iteration.

The values of the weights for the first iteration are randomly initialized between 0 and 1, while the values for the biases can be set to 0 initially. Once the first iteration is run, the values will be updated, so that the process can start again.

The activation function can be of different types. Some of the most common ones are the **Rectified Linear Unit (ReLU)**, the **Hyperbolic tangent (tanh)**, and the **Sigmoid** and **Softmax** functions, which will be explained in a subsequent section.

COST FUNCTION

Considering that the final objective of the training process is to build a model based on a given set of data that maps an expected output, it is particularly important to measure the model's ability to estimate a relation between **X** and **Y** by comparing the differences between the predicted value (**Y_hat**) and the ground truth (**Y**). This is accomplished by calculating the cost function (also known as the **loss function**) to determine how poor the model's predictions are. The cost function is calculated for each iteration to measure the progress of the model along the iteration process, with the objective of finding the values for the weights and biases that minimize the cost function.

For classification tasks, the cost function most commonly used is the **cross-entropy cost function**, where the higher the value of the cost function, the greater the divergence between the predicted and actual values.

For a binary classification task, that is, tasks with only two class output labels, the cross-entropy cost function is calculated as follows:

```
cost = -(y * log(y_hat) + (1-y) * (1-y_hat))
```

Here, y would be either 1 or 0 (either of the two class labels), y_{hat} would be the probability calculated by the model, and *log* would be the natural logarithm.

For a multiclass classification task, the formula is as follows:

$$cost = -\sum_{c=1}^{M} y_c * \log(y_{hat,c})$$

Figure 5.5: The cost function for a multiclass classification task

Here, *c* represents a class label and *M* refers to the total number of class labels.

Once the cost function is calculated, the training process proceeds to perform the backpropagation step, which will be explained in the following section.

Moreover, for regression tasks, the cost function would be the RMSE, which was explained in *Chapter 3, Supervised Learning – Key Steps*.

BACKPROPAGATION

The backpropagation procedure was introduced as part of the training process of ANNs to make learning faster. It basically involves calculating the partial derivatives of the cost function with respect to the weights and biases along the network. The objective of this is to minimize the cost function by changing the weights and the biases.

Considering that the weights and biases are not directly contained in the cost function, a chain rule is used to propagate the error from the cost function backward until it reaches the first layers of the network. Next, a weighted average of the derivatives is calculated, which is used as the value to update the weights and biases before running a new iteration.

There are several algorithms that can be used to perform backpropagation, but the most common one is **gradient descent**. Gradient descent is an optimization algorithm that tries to find some local or global minimum of a function, which, in this case, is the cost function. It does so by determining the direction in which the model should move to reduce the error.

For instance, the following diagram displays an example of the training process of an ANN through the different iterations, where the job of backpropagation is to determine the direction in which the weights and biases should be updated, so that the error can continue to be minimized until it reaches a minimum point:

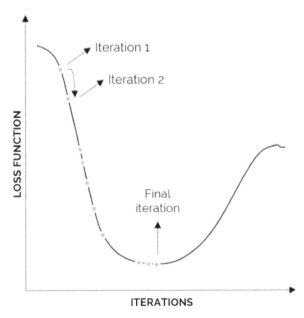

Figure 5.6: Example of the iterative process of training an ANN

It is important to highlight that backpropagation does not always find the global minima, since it stops updating once it has reached the lowest point in a slope, regardless of any other regions. For instance, consider the following diagram:

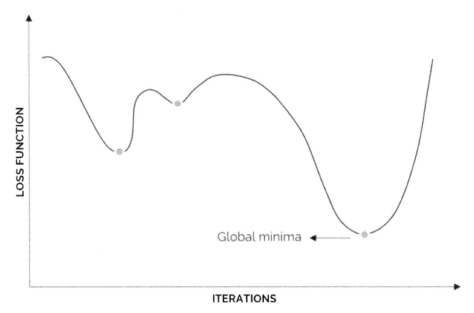

Figure 5.7: Examples of minimum points

Although all three points can be considered minimum points when compared to the points to their left and right, only one of them is the global minima.

UPDATING THE WEIGHTS AND BIASES

Taking the derivatives' average that was calculated during backpropagation, the final step of an iteration is to update the values of the weights and biases. This process is done using the following formula for updating weights and biases:

```
New weight = old weight - derivative rate * learning rate
New bias = old bias - derivative rate * learning rate
```

Here, the old values are those used to perform the forward propagation step, the derivative rate is the value obtained from the backpropagation step, which is different for the weights and the biases, and the learning rate is a constant that is used to neutralize the effect of the derivative rate, so that the changes in the weights and biases are small and smooth. This has been proven to help reach the lowest point more quickly.

Once the weights and the biases have been updated, the entire process starts again.

UNDERSTANDING THE HYPERPARAMETERS

Hyperparameters, as you have seen so far, are parameters that can be fine-tuned to improve the accuracy of a model. For neural networks, hyperparameters can be classified into two main groups:

- Those that alter the structure of the network

- Those that modify the process to train it

An important part of building an ANN is the process of fine-tuning the hyperparameters by performing error analysis and by playing around with the hyperparameters that help to solve the condition that is affecting the network. As a general reminder, networks suffering from high bias can usually be improved by creating bigger networks or training for longer durations of time (that is, more iterations), whereas networks suffering from high variance can benefit from the addition of more training data or by introducing a regularization technique, which will be explained in a subsequent section.

Considering that the number of hyperparameters that can be changed for training an ANN is large, the most commonly used ones will be explained in the following sections.

NUMBER OF HIDDEN LAYERS AND UNITS

The number of hidden layers and the number of units in each layer can be set by the researcher, as mentioned previously. Again, there is no exact science to select this number, and, on the contrary, the selection of this number is part of the fine-tuning process to test different approximations.

Nonetheless, when selecting the number of hidden layers, some data scientists lean toward an approach wherein multiple networks are trained, each with an extra layer. The model with the lowest error is the one with the correct number of hidden layers. Unfortunately, this approach does not always work well, as more complex data problems do not really show a difference in performance through simply changing the number of hidden layers, regardless of the other hyperparameters.

On the other hand, there are several techniques that you can use to choose the number of units in a hidden layer. It is common for data scientists to choose the initial values for both of these hyperparameters based on similar research papers that are available online. This means that a good starting point would be copying the architecture of networks that have been successfully used for projects in a similar field, and then, through error analysis, fine-tuning the hyperparameters to improve performance.

Nonetheless, it is important to consider the fact that based on research activity, deeper networks (networks with many hidden layers) outperform wider networks (networks with many units in each layer).

ACTIVATION FUNCTIONS

As mentioned previously, the activation function is used to introduce non-linearity to the model. The most commonly used activation functions are the following:

- **ReLU**: The output of this function is either 0 or the number derived from the linear function, whichever is higher. This means that the output will be the raw number it receives whenever this number is above 0, otherwise, the output would be 0.

- **Tanh**: This function consists of the division of the hyperbolic sine by the hyperbolic cosine of the input. The output is a number between -1 and 1.

- **Sigmoid**: The function has an S-shape. It takes the input and converts it into a probability. The output from this function is between 0 and 1.

- **Softmax**: Similar to the sigmoid function, this calculates the probability of the input, with the difference being that the Softmax function can be used for multiclass classification tasks as it is capable of calculating the probability of a class label in reference to the others.

The selection of an activation function should be done by considering that, conventionally, both the ReLU and the Hyperbolic tangent (tanh) activation functions are used for all of the hidden layers, with ReLU being the most popular one among scientists due to its performance in relation to the majority of data problems.

Moreover, the Sigmoid and the Softmax activation functions should be used for the output layer, as their outcome is in the form of a probability. The Sigmoid activation function is used for binary classification problems, as it only outputs the probability for two class labels, whereas the Softmax activation function can be used for either binary or multiclass classification problems.

REGULARIZATION

Regularization is a technique used in machine learning to improve a model that is suffering from overfitting, which means that this hyperparameter is mostly used when it is strictly required, and its main objective is to increase the generalization ability of the model.

There are different regularization techniques, but the most common ones are the L1, L2, and dropout techniques. Although scikit-learn only supports L2 for its MLP classifier, brief explanations of the three forms of regularization are as follows:

- The L1 and L2 techniques add a regularization term to the cost function as a way of penalizing high weights that may be affecting the performance of the model. The main difference between these approaches is that the regularization term for L1 is the absolute value of the magnitude of the weights, while for L2, it is the squared magnitude of the weights. For regular data problems, L2 has proven to work better, while L1 is mainly popular for feature extraction tasks since it creates sparse models.

- Dropout, on the other hand, refers to the model's ability to drop out some units in order to ignore their output during a step in the iteration, which simplifies the neural network. The dropout value is set between 0 and 1, and it represents the percentage of units that will be ignored. The units that are ignored are different in each iteration step.

BATCH SIZE

Another hyperparameter to be tuned during the construction of an ANN is the batch size. This refers to the number of instances to be fed to the neural network during an iteration, which will be used to perform a forward and a backward pass through the network. For the next iteration, a new set of instances will be used.

This technique also helps to improve the model's ability to generalize to the training data because, in each iteration, it is fed with new combinations of instances, which is useful when dealing with an overfitted model.

NOTE

As per the result of many years of research, a good practice is to set the batch size to a value that is a multiple of 2. Some of the most common values are 32, 64, 128, and 256.

LEARNING RATE

The learning rate, as explained previously, is introduced to help determine the size of the steps that the model will take to get to the local or global minima in each iteration. The lower the learning rate, the slower the learning process of the network, but this results in better models. On the other hand, the larger the learning rate, the faster the learning process of the model; however, this may result in a model not converging.

> **NOTE**
>
> The default learning rate value is usually set to 0.001.

NUMBER OF ITERATIONS

A neural network is trained through an iterative process, as mentioned previously. Therefore, it is necessary to set the number of iterations that the model will perform. The best way to set up the ideal number of iterations is to start low, between 200 and 500, and increase it, in the event that the plot of the cost function over each iteration shows a decreasing line. Needless to say, the larger the number of iterations, the longer it takes to train a model.

Additionally, increasing the number of iterations is a technique known to address underfitted networks. This is because it gives the network more time to find the right weights and biases that generalize to the training data.

APPLICATIONS OF NEURAL NETWORKS

In addition to the preceding architecture, a number of new architectures have emerged over time, thanks to the popularity of neural networks. Some of the most popular ones are **convolutional neural networks**, which can handle the processing of images by using filters as layers, and **recurrent neural networks**, which are used to process sequences of data such as text translations.

On account of this, the applications of neural networks extend to almost any data problem, ranging from simple to complex. While a neural network is capable of finding patterns in really large datasets (either for classification or regression tasks), they are also known for effectively handling challenging problems, such as the autonomous abilities of self-driving cars, the construction of chatbots, and the recognition of faces.

LIMITATIONS OF NEURAL NETWORKS

Some of the limitations of training neural networks are as follows:

- The training process takes time. Regardless of the hyperparameters used, they generally take time to converge.

- They need very large datasets in order to work better. Neural networks are meant for larger datasets, as their main advantage is their ability to find patterns within millions of values.

- They are considered a black box as there is no actual knowledge of how the network arrives at a result. Although the math behind the training process is clear, it is not possible to know what assumptions the model makes while being trained.

- The hardware requirements are large. Again, the greater the complexity of the problem, the larger the hardware requirements.

Although ANNs can be applied to almost any data problem, due to their limitations, it is always a good practice to test other algorithms when dealing with simpler data problems. This is important because applying neural networks to data problems that can be solved by simpler models makes the costs outweigh the benefits.

APPLYING AN ARTIFICIAL NEURAL NETWORK

Now that you know the components of an ANN, as well as the different steps that it follows to train a model and make predictions, let's train a simple network using the scikit-learn library.

In this topic, scikit-learn's neural network module will be used to train a network using the datasets used in the previous chapter's exercises and activities (that is, the Fertility Dataset and the Processed Census Income Dataset). It is important to mention that scikit-learn is not the most appropriate library for neural networks, as it does not currently support many types of neural networks, and its performance over deeper networks is not as good as other neural network specialized libraries, such as TensorFlow and PyTorch.

The neural network module in scikit-learn currently supports an MLP for classification, an MLP for regression, and a Restricted Boltzmann Machine architecture. Considering that the case study consists of a classification task, the MLP for classifications will be used.

SCIKIT-LEARN'S MULTILAYER PERCEPTRON

An MLP is a supervised learning algorithm that, as the name indicates, uses multiple layers (hidden layers) to learn a non-linear function that translates the input values into output, either for classification or regression. As we explained previously, the job of each unit of a layer is to transform the data received from the previous layer by calculating a linear function and then applying an activation function to break the linearity.

It is important to mention the fact that an MLP has a non-convex loss function that, as mentioned previously, signifies that there may be multiple local minima. This means that different initializations of the weights and biases will result in different trained models, which, in turn, indicates different accuracy levels.

The MLP classifier in scikit-learn has around 20 different hyperparameters associated with the architecture or the learning process, which can be altered in order to modify the training process of the network. Fortunately, all of these hyperparameters have set default values, which allows us to run an initial model without much effort. The results from this model can then be used to tune the hyperparameters as required.

To train an MLP classifier, it is required that you input two arrays: first, the **X** input of dimensions (**n_samples**, **n_features**) containing the training data, and then the **Y** input of dimensions (**n_sample**) that contains the label values for each sample.

Similar to the algorithms that we looked at in the previous chapter, the model is trained using the **fit** method, and then predictions can be obtained by using the **predict** method on the trained model.

EXERCISE 5.01: APPLYING THE MLP CLASSIFIER CLASS

In this exercise, you will train a model using scikit-learn's MLP to solve a classification task that consists of determining whether the fertility of the subjects has been affected by their demographics, their environmental conditions, and their previous medical conditions.

NOTE

For the exercises and activities within this chapter, you will need to have Python 3.7, NumPy, Jupyter, pandas, and scikit-learn installed on your system.

1. Open a Jupyter Notebook to implement this exercise. Import all the necessary elements to read the dataset and to calculate a model's accuracy, as well as scikit-learn's **MLPClassifier** class:

```
import pandas as pd
from sklearn.neural_network import MLPClassifier
from sklearn.metrics import accuracy_score
```

2. Using the Fertility Dataset from the previous chapter, read the **.csv** file. Make sure that you add the **header** argument equal to **None** to the **read_csv** function, considering that the dataset does not contain a header row:

```
data = pd.read_csv("fertility_Diagnosis.csv", header=None)
```

3. Split the dataset into **X** and **Y** sets in order to separate the features data from the label values:

```
X = data.iloc[:,:9]
Y = data.iloc[:,9]
```

4. Instantiate the **MLPClassifier** class from the **neural_network** module of scikit-learn and use the **fit** method to train a model. When instantiating the model, leave all the hyperparameters at their default values, but add a **random_state** argument equal to **101** to ensure that you get the same results as the one shown in this exercise:

```
model = MLPClassifier(random_state=101)
model = model.fit(X, Y)
```

Address the warning that appears after running the **fit** method:

```
/home/daniel/Desktop/VirtualEnvs/explore_data/lib/python3.6/site-packages/sklearn/neural_network/multilayer_perceptron.p
y:562: ConvergenceWarning: Stochastic Optimizer: Maximum iterations (200) reached and the optimization hasn't converged
yet.
  % self.max_iter, ConvergenceWarning)
```

Figure 5.8: Warning message displayed after running the fit method

As you can see, the warning specifies that after running the default number of iterations, which is **200**, the model has not reached convergence.

5. To address this issue, try higher values for the iterations until the warning stops appearing. To change the number of iterations, add the **max_iter** argument inside the parentheses during the instantiation of the model:

```
model = MLPClassifier(random_state=101, max_iter =1200)
model = model.fit(X, Y)
```

Furthermore, the output beneath the warning explains the values used for all of the hyperparameters of the MLP.

6. Finally, perform a prediction by using the model that you trained previously, for a new instance with the following values for each feature: **−0.33, 0.69, 0, 1, 1, 0, 0.8, 0, 0.88**.

Use the following code:

```
pred = model.predict([[-0.33,0.69,0,1,1,0,0.8,0,0.88]])
print(pred)
```

The model's prediction is equal to **N**, that is, the model predicts the person with the specified features to have a normal diagnosis.

7. Calculate the accuracy of your model, based on the predictions it achieves over the **X** variable, as follows:

```
pred = model.predict(X)
score = accuracy_score(Y, pred)
print(score)
```

The accuracy of your model is equal to **98%**.

> **NOTE**
>
> To access the source code for this specific section, please refer to https://packt.live/2BaKHRe.
>
> You can also run this example online at https://packt.live/37tTxpv. You must execute the entire Notebook in order to get the desired result.

You have successfully trained and evaluated the performance of an MLP model.

ACTIVITY 5.01: TRAINING AN MLP FOR OUR CENSUS INCOME DATASET

With the objective of comparing the performance of the algorithms trained in the previous chapter with the performance of a neural network, for this activity, we will continue to work with the Preprocessed Census Income Dataset. Consider the following scenario: your company is continually offering a course for employees to improve their abilities, and you have recently learned about neural networks and their power. You have decided to build a network to model the dataset that you were given previously in order to test whether a neural network is better at predicting a person's income based on their demographic data.

NOTE

Start this activity using the preprocessed dataset from the previous chapter: **census_income_dataset_preprocessed.csv**. You can also find the preprocessed dataset on this book's GitHub repository at https://packt.live/2UQIthA.

Perform the following steps to complete this activity:

1. Import all the elements required to load and split a dataset, train an MLP, and to measure accuracy.

2. Using the preprocessed Census Income Dataset, separate the features from the target, creating the variables **X** and **Y**.

3. Divide the dataset into training, validation, and testing sets, using a split ratio of 10%.

    NOTE

    Remember to continue using a **random_state** argument equal to **101** when performing the dataset split in order to set a seed to arrive at the same results as the ones in this book.

4. Instantiate the **MLPClassifier** class from scikit-learn and train the model with the training data.

    Leave all the hyperparameters at their default values. Again, use a **random_state** equal to 101.

    Although a warning will appear specifying that, with the given iterations, no convergence was reached, leave the warning unaddressed, since hyperparameter fine-tuning will be explored in the following sections of this chapter.

5. Calculate the accuracy of the model for all three sets (training, validation, and testing).

    NOTE

    The solution to this activity can be found on page 240.

The accuracy score for the three sets should be as follows:

Train sets = 0.8465

Dev sets = 0.8246

Test sets = 0.8415

PERFORMANCE ANALYSIS

In the following section, we will first perform error analysis using the accuracy metric as a tool to determine the condition that is affecting (in greater proportion) the performance of the algorithm. Once the model is diagnosed, the hyperparameters can be tuned to improve the overall performance of the algorithm. The final model will be compared to those that were created during the previous chapter in order to determine whether a neural network outperforms the other models.

ERROR ANALYSIS

Using the accuracy score calculated in *Activity 5.01, Training an MLP for Our Census Income Dataset*, we can calculate the error rates for each of the sets and compare them against one another to diagnose the condition that is affecting the model. To do so, a Bayes error equal to 1% will be assumed, considering that other models in the previous chapter were able to achieve an accuracy level of over 97%:

	Accuracy score	Error rate	Difference
Bayes error		0.01	
Training sets	0.8465	0.1535	0.1435
Validation sets	0.8246	0.1754	0.0219
Testing sets	0.8415	0.1585	-0.0169

Figure 5.9: Accuracy score and error rate of the network

NOTE

Considering *Figure 5.9*, remember that in order to detect the condition that is affecting the network, it is necessary to take an error rate and, from that, subtract the value of the error rate above it. The biggest positive difference is the one that we use to diagnose the model.

According to the column of differences, it is evident that the biggest difference is found between the error rate in the training set and the Bayes error. Based on this, it is possible to conclude that the model is suffering from *high bias*, which, as explained in previous chapters, can be handled by training a bigger network and/or training for longer periods of time (a higher number of iterations).

HYPERPARAMETER FINE-TUNING

Through error analysis, it was possible to determine that the network is suffering from high bias. This is highly important as it indicates the actions that need to be taken in order to improve the performance of the model in greater proportion.

Considering that both the number of iterations and the size of the network (number of layers and units) should be changed using a trial-and-error approach, the following experiments will be performed:

	Default values	Experiment 1	Experiment 2	Experiment 3
Number of iterations	200	500	500	500
Number of hidden layers	1	1	2	3
Number of units per layer	100	100	100,100	100,100,100

Figure 5.10: Suggested experiments to tune the hyperparameters

NOTE

Some experiments may take longer to run due to their complexity. For instance, Experiment 3 will take longer than Experiment 2.

The idea behind these experiments is to be able to test different values for the different hyperparameters in order to find out whether an improvement can be achieved. If the improvements achieved through these experiments are significant, further experiments should be considered.

Similar to adding the **random_state** argument to the initialization of the MLP, the change in the values of the number of iterations and the size of the network can be achieved using the following code, which shows the values for Experiment 3:

```
from sklearn.neural_network import MLPClassifier
model = MLPClassifier(random_state=101, max_iter = 500, \
                      hidden_layer_sizes=(100,100,100))
model = model.fit(X_train, Y_train)
```

> **NOTE**
>
> To find what term to use in order to change each hyperparameter, visit scikit-learn's **MLPClassifier** page at http://scikit-learn.org/stable/modules/generated/sklearn.neural_network.MLPClassifier.html.

As you can see in the preceding snippet, the **max_iter** argument is used to set the number of iterations to run during the training of the network. The **hidden_layer_sizes** argument is used to both set the number of hidden layers and set the number of units in each. For instance, in the preceding example, by setting the argument to **(100,100,100)**, the architecture of the network is of 3 hidden layers, each with 100 units. Of course, this architecture also includes the required input and output layers.

> **NOTE**
>
> Using the example to train a network with the configurations of Experiment 3, you are encouraged to try to execute the training process for the configurations of Experiment 1 and 2.

The accuracy scores from running the preceding experiments can be seen in the following table:

	Initial model	Experiment 1	Experiment 2	Experiment 3
Training sets	0.8465	0.8243	0.8673	0.8494
Validation sets	0.8246	0.8031	0.8311	0.8299
Testing sets	0.8415	0.8222	0.8520	0.8428

Figure 5.11: Accuracy scores for all experiments

> **NOTE**
>
> Keep in mind that the main purpose behind tuning the hyperparameters is to decrease the difference between the error rate of the training set and the Bayes error, which is why most of the analysis is done by considering only this value.

Through an analysis of the accuracy scores of the experiments, it can be concluded that the best configuration of hyperparameters is the one used during Experiment 2. Additionally, it is possible to conclude that there is most likely no point in trying other values for the number of iterations, considering that increasing the number of iterations did not have a positive effect on the performance of the algorithm.

Nonetheless, in order to test the width of the hidden layers, the following experiments will be considered, using the selected values for the number of iterations and the number of hidden layers of Experiment 2, but varying the number of units in each layer:

	Initial model (Experiment 2)	Experiment 2.1	Experiment 2.2
Number of iterations	500	500	500
Number of hidden layers	2	2	2
Number of units per layer	100,100	50,50	150,150

Figure 5.12: Suggested experiments to vary the width of the network

The accuracy score of the two experiments is shown, followed by an explanation of the logic behind them:

	Initial model (Experiment 2)	**Experiment 2 .1**	**Experiment 2.2**
Training sets	0.8673	0.8523	0.8590
Validation sets	0.8311	0.8289	0.8219
Testing sets	0.8520	0.8443	0.8455

Figure 5.13: Accuracy scores for the second round of experiments

It can be seen that the accuracy for both experiments decreases for all sets of data, in comparison to the initial model. By observing these values, it can be concluded that the performance of Experiment 2 is the highest in terms of testing sets, which leaves us with a network that iterates for 500 steps, with one input and output layer and two hidden layers with 100 units each.

> **NOTE**
>
> There is no ideal way to test the different configurations of hyperparameters. The only important thing to consider is that the focus is centered on those hyperparameters that solve the condition that is affecting the network in a greater proportion. Feel free to try more experiments if you wish.

Considering the accuracy scores of all three sets of Experiment 2 to calculate the error rate, the biggest difference is still between the training set error and the Bayes error. This means that the model may not be the best fit for the dataset, considering that the training set error could not be brought closer to the minimum possible error margin.

> **NOTE**
>
> To access the source code for this specific section, please refer to https://packt.live/3e2O8bS.
>
> This section does not currently have an online interactive example, and will need to be run locally.

MODEL COMPARISON

When more than one model has been trained, the final step related to the process of creating a model is a comparison between the models in order to choose the one that best represents the training data in a generalized way, so that it works well over unseen data.

The comparison, as mentioned previously, must be done by using only the metric that was selected to measure the performance of the models for the data problem. This is important, considering that one model can perform very differently for each metric, so the model that maximizes the performance with the ideal metric should be selected.

Although the metric is calculated on all three sets of data (training, validation, and testing) in order to be able to perform error analysis, for most cases, comparison and selection should be done by prioritizing the results obtained with the testing set. This is mainly due to the purpose of the sets, considering that the training set is used to create the model, the validation set is used to fine-tune the hyperparameters, and finally, the testing set is used to measure the overall performance of the model on unseen data.

Taking this into account, the model with a superior performance on the testing set, after having improved all models to their fullest potential, will be the one that performs best on unseen data.

ACTIVITY 5.02: COMPARING DIFFERENT MODELS TO CHOOSE THE BEST FIT FOR THE CENSUS INCOME DATA PROBLEM

Consider the following scenario: after training four different models with the available data, you have been asked to perform an analysis to choose the model that best suits the case study.

> **NOTE**
>
> The following activity is mainly analytical. Use the results obtained from the activities in the previous chapter, as well as the activity in the current chapter.

Perform the following steps to compare the different models:

1. Open the Jupyter Notebooks that you used to train the models.

2. Compare the four models, based only on their accuracy scores. Fill in the details in the following table:

	Naïve Bayes	Decision Tree	SVM	Multilayer Perceptron
Training sets				
Validation sets				
Testing sets				

Figure 5.14: Accuracy scores of all four models for the Census Income Dataset

3. On the basis of the accuracy scores, identify the model with the best performance.

> **NOTE**
>
> The solution to this activity can be found on page 242.

SUMMARY

This chapter mainly focused on ANNs (the MLP, in particular), which have become increasingly important in the field of machine learning due to their ability to tackle highly complex data problems that usually use extremely large datasets with patterns that are impossible to see with the human eye.

The main objective is to emulate the architecture of the human brain by using mathematical functions to process data. The process that is used to train an ANN consists of a forward propagation step, the calculation of a cost function, a backpropagation step, and the updating of the different weights and biases that help to map the input values to an output.

In addition to the variables of the weights and biases, ANNs have multiple hyperparameters that can be tuned to improve the performance of the network, which can be done by modifying the architecture or training process of the algorithm. Some of the most popular hyperparameters are the size of the network (in terms of hidden layers and units), the number of iterations, the regularization term, the batch size, and the learning rate.

Once these concepts were covered, we created a simple network to tackle the Census Income Dataset problem that was introduced in the previous chapter. Next, by performing error analysis, we fine-tuned some of the hyperparameters of the network to improve its performance.

In the next chapter, we will learn how to develop an end-to-end machine learning solution, starting from the understanding of the data and training of the model, as seen thus far, and ending with the process of saving a trained model in order to be able to make future use of it.

6

BUILDING YOUR OWN PROGRAM

OVERVIEW

In this chapter, we will present all the steps required to solve a problem using machine learning. We will take a look at the key stages involved in building a comprehensive program. We will save a model in order to get the same results every time it is run and call a saved model to use it for predictions on unseen data. By the end of this chapter, you will be able to create an interactive version of your program so that anyone can use it effectively.

INTRODUCTION

In the previous chapters, we covered the main concepts of machine learning, beginning with the distinction between the two main learning approaches (supervised and unsupervised learning), and then moved on to the specifics of some of the most popular algorithms in the data science community.

This chapter will talk about the importance of building complete machine learning programs, rather than just training models. This will involve taking the models to the next level, where they can be accessed and used easily.

We will do this by learning how to save a trained model. This will allow the best performing model to be loaded in order to make predictions over unseen data. We will also learn the importance of making a saved model available through platforms where users can easily interact with it.

This is especially important when working in a team, either for a company or for research purposes, as it allows all members of the team to use the model without needing a full understanding of it.

PROGRAM DEFINITION

The following section will cover the key stages required to construct a comprehensive machine learning program that allows easy access to the trained model so that we can perform predictions for all future data. These stages will be applied to the construction of a program that allows a bank to determine the promotional strategy for a financial product in its marketing campaign.

BUILDING A PROGRAM – KEY STAGES

At this point, you should be able to pre-process a dataset, build different models using training data, and compare those models in order to choose the one that best fits the data at hand. These are some of the processes that are handled during the first two stages of building a program, which ultimately allows the creation of the model. Nonetheless, a program should also consider the process of saving the final model, as well as the ability to perform quick predictions without the need for coding.

The processes that we just discussed are divided into three main stages and will be explained in the following sections. These stages represent the foremost requirements of any machine learning project.

PREPARATION

Preparation consists of all the procedures that we have developed thus far, with the objective of outlining the project in alignment with the available information and the desired outcome. The following is a brief description of the three processes in this stage (these have been discussed in detail in previous chapters):

1. **Data Exploration**: Once the objective of the study has been established, data exploration is undertaken in order to understand the data that is available and to obtain valuable insights. These insights will be used later to make decisions regarding pre-processing and dividing the data and selecting models, among other uses. The information that's most commonly obtained during data exploration includes the size of the dataset (number of instances and features), the irrelevant features, and whether missing values or evident outliers are present.

2. **Data Pre-processing**: As we have already discussed, data pre-processing primarily refers to the process of handling missing values, outliers, and noisy data; converting qualitative features into their numeric forms; and normalizing or standardizing these values. This process can be done manually in any data editor, such as Excel, or by using libraries to code the procedure.

3. **Data Splitting**: The final process, data splitting, involves splitting the entire dataset into two or three sets (depending on the approach) that will be used for training, validating, and testing the overall performance of the model. Separating the features and the class label is also handled during this stage.

CREATION

This stage involves all of the steps that are required to create a model that fits the data that is available. This can be done by selecting different algorithms, training and tuning them, comparing the performance of each, and, finally, selecting the one that generalizes best to the data (meaning that it achieves better overall performance). The processes in this stage will be discussed briefly, as follows:

1. **Algorithm Selection**: Irrespective of whether you decide to choose one or multiple algorithms, it is crucial to select an algorithm on the basis of the available data and to take the advantages of each algorithm into consideration. This is important since many data scientists make the mistake of choosing neural networks for any data problem when, in reality, simpler problems can be tackled using simpler models that run more quickly and perform better with smaller datasets.

2. **Training Process**: This process involves training the model using the training dataset. This means that the algorithm uses the features data ($\mathbf{X}$) and the label classes ($\mathbf{Y}$) to determine relationship patterns that will help generalize to unseen data and make predictions when the class label is not available.

3. **Model Evaluation**: This process is handled by measuring the performance of the algorithm through the metric that's been selected for the study. As we mentioned previously, it is important to choose the metric that best represents the purpose of the study, considering that the same model can do very well in terms of one metric and poorly in terms of another.

   While evaluating the model on the validation set, hyperparameters are fine-tuned to achieve the best possible performance. Once the hyperparameters have been tuned, the evaluation is performed on the testing set to measure the overall performance of the model on unseen data.

4. **Model Comparison and Selection**: When multiple models are created based on different algorithms, a model comparison is performed to select the one that outperforms the others. This comparison should be done by using the same metric for all the models.

INTERACTION

The final stage in building a comprehensive machine learning program consists of allowing the final user to easily interact with the model. This includes the process of saving the model into a file, calling the file that holds the saved model, and developing a channel through which users can interact with the model:

1. **Storing the Final Model**: This process is introduced during the development of a machine learning program as it is crucial to enable the unaltered use of the model for future predictions. The process of saving the model is highly important, considering that most algorithms are randomly initialized each time they are run, which makes the results different for each run. The process of saving the model will be explained further later in this chapter.

2. **Loading the Model**: Once the model has been saved in a file, it can be accessed by loading the file into any code. The model is then stored in a variable that can be used to apply the `predict` method on unseen data. This process will also be explained later in this chapter.

3. **Channel of Interaction**: Finally, it is crucial to develop an interactive and easy way to perform predictions using the saved model, especially because, on many occasions, models are created by the technology team for other teams to use. This means that an ideal program should allow non-experts to use the model for predicting by simply typing in the input data. This idea will also be expanded upon later in this chapter.

The following diagram illustrates the preceding stages:

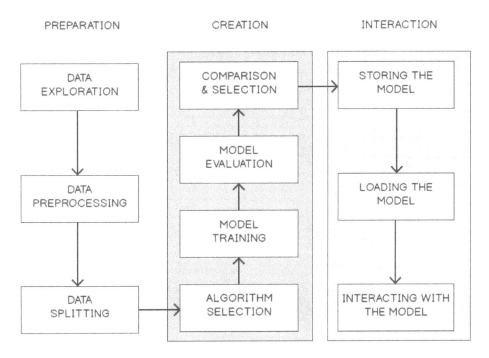

Figure 6.1: Stages for building a machine learning program

The rest of this chapter will focus on the final stage of building a model (the interaction), considering that all the previous steps were discussed in previous chapters.

UNDERSTANDING THE DATASET

To learn how to implement the processes in the *Interaction* section, we will build a program that's capable of predicting whether a person will be interested in investing in a term deposit, which will help the bank target its promotion efforts. A term deposit is money that is deposited into a banking institution that cannot be withdrawn for a specific period of time.

The dataset that was used to build this program is available in the UC Irvine Machine Learning Repository under the name **Bank Marketing Dataset**.

> **NOTE**
>
> To download this dataset, visit the following link: http://archive.ics.uci.edu/ml/datasets/Bank+Marketing.
>
> The dataset is also available in this book's GitHub repository: https://packt.live/2wnJyny.
>
> Citation: [Moro et al., 2014] S. Moro, P. Cortez and P. Rita. *A Data-Driven Approach to Predict the Success of Bank Telemarketing.* Decision Support Systems, Elsevier, 62:22-31, June 2014.

Once you have accessed the link of the UC Irvine Machine Learning repository, follow these steps to download the dataset:

1. First, click on the `Data Folder` link.

2. Click the **bank** hyperlink to trigger the download

3. Open the `.zip` folder and extract the `bank-full.csv` file.

   In this section, we will perform a quick exploration of the dataset in a Jupyter Notebook. However, in *Activity 6.01, Performing the Preparation and Creation Stages for the Bank Marketing Dataset*, you will be encouraged to perform a good exploration and pre-process the dataset to arrive at a better mode.

4. Import the required libraries:

```
import pandas as pd
import numpy as np
```

5. As we have learned thus far, the dataset can be loaded into a Jupyter Notebook using Pandas:

```
data = pd.read_csv("bank-full.csv")
data.head()
```

The preceding code reads all the features for one instance in a single column, since the **read_csv** function uses commas as the default delimiter for columns, while the dataset uses semicolons as the delimiter, as can be seen by displaying the head of the resulting DataFrame.

> **NOTE**
>
> The delimiter refers to the character that's used to split a string into columns. For instance, a comma-delimited file is one that separates text into columns on the appearances of commas.

The DataFrame will look as follows:

	age;"job";"marital";"education";"default";"balance";"housing";"loan";"contact";"day";"month";"duration";"campaign";"pdays";"previous";"poutcome";"y"
0	58;"management";"married";"tertiary";"no";2143...
1	44;"technician";"single";"secondary";"no";29;"...
2	33;"entrepreneur";"married";"secondary";"no";2...
3	47;"blue-collar";"married";"unknown";"no";1506...
4	33;"unknown";"single";"unknown";"no";1;"no";"n...

Figure 6.2: Screenshot of the data in the .csv file before splitting the data into columns

This can be fixed by adding the **delimiter** parameter to the **read_csv** function and defining the semicolon as the delimiter, as shown in the following code snippet:

```
data = pd.read_csv("bank-full.csv", delimiter = ";")
data.head()
```

After this step, the data should look as follows:

	age	job	marital	education	default	balance	housing	loan	contact	day	month	duration	campaign	pdays	previous	poutcome	y
0	58	management	married	tertiary	no	2143	yes	no	unknown	5	may	261	1	-1	0	unknown	no
1	44	technician	single	secondary	no	29	yes	no	unknown	5	may	151	1	-1	0	unknown	no
2	33	entrepreneur	married	secondary	no	2	yes	yes	unknown	5	may	76	1	-1	0	unknown	no
3	47	blue-collar	married	unknown	no	1506	yes	no	unknown	5	may	92	1	-1	0	unknown	no
4	33	unknown	single	unknown	no	1	no	no	unknown	5	may	198	1	-1	0	unknown	no

Figure 6.3: Screenshot of the data in the .csv file after splitting it into columns

As shown in the preceding screenshot, the file contains unknown values that should be handled as missing values.

6. To aid the process of dealing with missing values, all unknown values will be replaced by **NaN** using Pandas' `replace` function, as well as NumPy, as follows:

```
data = data.replace("unknown", np.NaN)
data.head()
```

By printing the head of the **data** variable, the output of the preceding code snippet is as follows:

	age	job	marital	education	default	balance	housing	loan	contact	day	month	duration	campaign	pdays	previous	poutcome	y
0	58	management	married	tertiary	no	2143	yes	no	NaN	5	may	261	1	-1	0	NaN	no
1	44	technician	single	secondary	no	29	yes	no	NaN	5	may	151	1	-1	0	NaN	no
2	33	entrepreneur	married	secondary	no	2	yes	yes	NaN	5	may	76	1	-1	0	NaN	no
3	47	blue-collar	married	NaN	no	1506	yes	no	NaN	5	may	92	1	-1	0	NaN	no
4	33	NaN	single	NaN	no	1	no	no	NaN	5	may	198	1	-1	0	NaN	no

Figure 6.4: Screenshot of the data in the .csv file after replacing unknown values

This will allow us to easily handle missing values during the pre-processing of the dataset.

7. Finally, the edited dataset is saved in a new **.csv** file so that it can be used for the activities throughout this chapter. You can do this by using the **to_csv** function, as follows:

```
data.to_csv("bank-full-dataset.csv")
```

> **NOTE**
>
> To access the source code for this specific section, please refer to https://packt.live/2AAX2ym.
>
> You can also run this example online at https://packt.live/3ftYXnf. You must execute the entire Notebook in order to get the desired result.

The file should contain a total of 45,211 instances, each with 16 features and one class label, which can be verified by printing the shape of the variable holding the dataset. The class label is binary, of the **yes** or **no** type, and indicates whether the client subscribes to a term deposit with the bank.

Each instance represents a client of the bank, while the features capture demographic information, as well as data regarding the nature of the contact with the client during the current (and previous) promotional campaign.

The following table displays brief descriptions of all 16 features. This will help you determine the relevance of each feature to the study, and will provide an idea of some of the steps required to pre-process the data:

Name	Type	Description
age	Quantitative (continuous)	The age of the individual.
job	Qualitative (nominal)	The type of job the individual currently has. For instance: "blue-collar".
marital	Qualitative (nominal)	The marital status of the individual.
education	Qualitative (ordinal)	The highest education level achieved by the individual.
default	Qualitative (nominal - binary)	Whether the individual has credit by default
balance	Quantitative (continuous)	Average yearly balance of the individual in euros.
housing	Qualitative (nominal - binary)	Whether the individual has any housing loan.
loan	Qualitative (nominal - binary)	Whether the individual has any personal loan.
contact	Qualitative (nominal)	The mode of communication used to contact the individual for the current campaign.
day	Quantitative (discrete)	The day of the month when the individual was last contacted for the current campaign.
month	Qualitative (nominal)	The month of the year when the individual was last contacted for the current campaign.
duration	Quantitative (continuous)	The duration, in seconds, of the last contact with the individual for the current campaign.
campaign	Quantitative (continuous)	The number of times the individual was contacted during the promotion campaign.
pdays	Quantitative (continuous)	The number of days that passed by after the individual was contacted for a previous campaign. The value -1 means that the client was not contacted for a previous campaign.
previous	Quantitative (continuous)	The number of times the individual was contacted for previous campaigns.
poutcome	Qualitative (nominal)	The outcome obtained from the previous campaign.

Figure 6.5: A table describing the features of the dataset

> **NOTE**
>
> You can find the preceding descriptions and more in this book's GitHub repository, in the folder named **Chapter06**. The file for the preceding example is named **bank-names.txt** and can be found in the **.zip** folder called **bank.zip**.

Using the information we obtained while exploring the dataset, it is possible to proceed with pre-processing the data and training the model, which will be the purpose of the following activity.

ACTIVITY 6.01: PERFORMING THE PREPARATION AND CREATION STAGES FOR THE BANK MARKETING DATASET

The objective of this activity is to perform the processes in the *preparation* and *creation* stages to build a comprehensive machine learning problem.

> **NOTE**
>
> For the exercises and activities within this chapter, you will need to have Python 3.7, NumPy, Jupyter, Pandas, and scikit-learn installed on your system.

Let's consider the following scenario: you work at the principal bank in your town, and the marketing team has decided that they want to know in advance if a client is likely to subscribe to a term deposit so that they can focus their efforts on targeting those clients.

For this, you have been provided with a dataset containing the details of current and previous marketing activities carried out by the team (the Bank Marketing Dataset that you have downloaded and explored). You have been asked to pre-process the dataset and compare two models so that you can select the best one.

Follow these steps to achieve this:

1. Open a Jupyter Notebook to implement this activity and import all the required elements.

2. Load the dataset into the notebook. Make sure that you load the one that was edited previously, named **bank-full-dataset.csv**, which is also available at https://packt.live/2wnJyny.

3. Select the metric that is the most appropriate for measuring the performance of the model, considering that the purpose of the study is to detect clients who are likely to subscribe to the term deposit.

4. Pre-process the dataset.

   Note that one of the qualitative features is ordinal, which is why it must be converted into a numeric form that follows the respective order. Use the following code snippet to do so:

```
data["education"] = data["education"].fillna["unknown"]
encoder = ["unknown", "primary", "secondary", "tertiary"]

for i, word in enumerate(encoder):
    data["education"] = data["education"].\
                        str.replace(word,str(i))
    data["education"] = data["education"].astype("int64")
```

5. Separate the features from the class label and split the dataset into three sets (training, validation, and testing).

6. Use the decision tree algorithm on the dataset and train the model.

7. Use the multilayer perceptron algorithm on the dataset and train the model.

> **NOTE**
>
> You can also try this with the other classification algorithms we discussed in this book. However, these two have been chosen so that you are also able to compare the difference in training times.

8. Evaluate both models by using the metric that you selected previously.

9. Fine-tune some of the hyperparameters to fix the issues you detected while evaluating the model by performing error analysis.

10. Compare the final versions of your models and select the one that you believe best fits the data.

Expected output:

	Decision Tree	Multilayer Perception
Training sets	0.61	0.76
Validation sets	0.57	0.60
Testing sets	0.54	0.55

Figure 6.6: Expected output

> **NOTE**
>
> You can find the solution for this activity on page 244.

SAVING AND LOADING A TRAINED MODEL

Although the process of manipulating a dataset and training the right model is crucial for developing a machine learning project, the work does not end there. Knowing how to save a trained model is key as this will allow you to save the hyperparameters, as well as the values for the weights and biases of your final model, so that it remains unchanged when it is run again.

Moreover, after the model has been saved to a file, it is also important to know how to load the saved model in order to use it to make predictions on new data. By saving and loading a model, we allow for the model to be reused at any moment and through many different means.

SAVING A MODEL

The process of saving a model is also called **serialization**, and it has become increasingly important due to the popularity of neural networks that use many parameters (weights and biases) that are randomly initialized every time the model is trained, as well as due to the introduction of bigger and more complex datasets that make the training process last for days, weeks, and sometimes months.

Considering this, the process of saving a model helps to optimize the use of machine learning solutions by standardizing the results to the saved version of the model. It also saves time as it allows you to directly apply the saved model to new data, without the need for retraining.

There are two main ways to save a trained model, one of which will be explained in this section. The `pickle` module is the standard way to serialize objects in Python, and it works by implementing a powerful algorithm that serializes the model and then saves it as a `.pkl` file.

> **NOTE**
>
> The other module that's available for saving a trained model is `joblib`, which is part of the SciPy ecosystem.

However, take into account that models are only saved when they are meant to be used in future projects or for future predictions. When a machine learning project is developed to understand the current data, there is no need to save it as the analysis will be performed after the model has been trained.

EXERCISE 6.01: SAVING A TRAINED MODEL

For the following exercise, we will use the Fertility Dataset that we downloaded in *Chapter 5*, *Artificial Neural Networks: Predicting Annual Income*. A neural network will be trained over the training data, and then saved. Follow these steps to complete this exercise:

> **NOTE**
>
> The dataset is also available in this book's GitHub repository:
> https://packt.live/2zBW84e.

1. Open a Jupyter Notebook to implement this exercise and import all the required elements to load a dataset, train a multilayer perceptron, and save a trained model:

```
import pandas as pd
from sklearn.neural_network import MLPClassifier
import pickle
import os
```

The **pickle** module, as explained previously, will be used to save the trained model. The **os** module is used to locate the current working directory of the Jupyter Notebook in order to save the model in the same path.

2. Load the Fertility dataset and split the data into a features matrix, **X**, and a target matrix, **Y**. Use the **header = None** argument, since the dataset does not have a header row:

```
data = pd.read_csv("fertility_Diagnosis.csv", header=None)

X = data.iloc[:,:9]
Y = data.iloc[:,9]
```

3. Train a multilayer perceptron classifier over the data. Set the number of iterations to **1200** to avoid getting a warning message indicating that the default number of iterations is insufficient to achieve convergence:

```
model = MLPClassifier(max_iter = 1200)
model.fit(X,Y)
```

> **NOTE**
>
> As a reminder, the output from calling the **fit** method consists of the model currently being trained with all the parameters that it takes in.

4. Serialize the model and save it in a file named **model_exercise.pkl**. Use the following code to do so:

```
path = os.getcwd() + "/model_exercise.pkl"
file = open(path, "wb")
pickle.dump(model, file)
```

In the preceding snippet, the **path** variable contains the path to the file that will hold the serialized model, where the first element locates the current working directory and the second element defines the name of the file to be saved. The **file** variable is used to create a file that will be saved in the desired path and has the file mode set to **wb**, which stands for **write** and **binary** (this is the way the serialized model must be written). Finally, the **dump** method is applied over the **pickle** module. It takes the model that was created previously, serializes it, and then saves it.

> **NOTE**
>
> To access the source code for this specific section, please refer to https://packt.live/3e18vWw.
>
> You can also run this example online at https://packt.live/2B7NJpC.
> You must execute the entire Notebook in order to get the desired result.

You have successfully saved a trained model. In the next section, we will be looking at loading a saved model.

LOADING A MODEL

The process of loading a model is also known as **deserialization**, and it consists of taking the previously saved file, deserializing it, and then loading it into code or Terminal so that you can use the model on new data. The **pickle** module is also used to load the model.

It is worth mentioning that the model does not need to be loaded in the same code file where it was trained and saved; on the contrary, it is meant to be loaded in any other file. This is mainly because the **load** method of the **pickle** library will return the model in a variable that will be used to apply the **predict** method.

When loading a model, it is important to not only import the **pickle** and **os** modules like we did before, but also the class of the algorithm that is used to train the model. For instance, to load a neural network model, it is necessary to import the **MLPClassifier** class, from the **neural_network** module of scikit-learn.

EXERCISE 6.02: LOADING A SAVED MODEL

In this exercise, using a different Jupyter Notebook, we will load the previously trained model (*Exercise 6.01*, *Saving a Trained Model*) and perform a prediction. Follow these steps to complete this exercise:

1. Open a Jupyter Notebook to implement this exercise.

2. Import the **pickle** and **os** modules. Also, import the **MLPCLassifier** class:

```
import pickle
import os
from sklearn.neural_network import MLPClassifier
```

The **pickle** module, as explained previously, will be used to load the trained model. The **os** module is used to locate the current working directory of the Jupyter Notebook in order to find the file containing the saved model.

3. Use **pickle** to load the saved model, as follows:

```
path = os.getcwd() + "/model_exercise.pkl"
file = open(path, "rb")
model = pickle.load(file)
```

Here, the **path** variable is used to store the path to the file containing the saved model. Next, the **file** variable is used to open the file using the **rb** file mode, which stands for **read** and **binary**. Finally, the **load** method is applied on the **pickle** module to deserialize and load the model into the **model** variable.

4. Use the loaded model to make a prediction for an individual, with the following values as the values for the features: **-0.33, 0.67, 1, 1, 0, 0, 0.8, -1, 0.5**.

Store the output obtained by applying the **predict** method to the **model** variable, in a variable named **pred**:

```
pred = model.predict([[-0.33,0.67,1,1,0,0,0.8,-1,0.5]])
print(pred)
```

By printing the **pred** variable, we get the value of the prediction to be equal to **0**, which means that the individual has an altered diagnosis, as shown here:

```
['0']
```

You have successfully loaded a saved model.

> **NOTE**
>
> To access the source code for this specific section, please refer to https://packt.live/2MXyGS7.
>
> You can also run this example online at https://packt.live/3dYgVxL. You must execute the entire Notebook in order to get the desired result.

ACTIVITY 6.02: SAVING AND LOADING THE FINAL MODEL FOR THE BANK MARKETING DATASET

Consider the following scenario: you have to save the model you created using the Bank Marketing Dataset so that it can be used in the future without the need to retrain the model and without the risk of getting different results each time. For this purpose, you need to save and load the model that you created in *Activity 6.01, Performing the Preparation and Creation Stages for the Bank Marketing Dataset*.

> **NOTE**
>
> The following activity will be divided into two parts.
>
> The first part carries out the process of saving the model and will be performed using the same Jupyter Notebook from *Activity 6.01, Performing the Preparation and Creation Stages for the Bank Marketing Dataset*. The second part consists of loading the saved model, which will be done using a different Jupyter Notebook.

Follow these steps to complete this activity:

1. Open the Jupyter Notebook from *Activity 6.01, Performing the Preparation and Creation Stages for the Bank Marketing Dataset*.

2. For learning purposes, take the model that you selected as the best model, remove the **random_state** argument, and run it a couple of times.

   Make sure that you run the calculation of the precision metric every time you run the model in order to see the difference in performance that's achieved with every run. Feel free to stop when you think you have landed at a model with good performance out of all the results you get from previous runs.

   > **NOTE**
   >
   > The results obtained in this book use a **random_state** of 2.

3. Save the model that you choose as the best performing one in a file named **final_model.pkl**.

   > **NOTE**
   >
   > Make sure that you use the **os** module to save the model in the same path as the current Jupyter Notebook.

4. Open a new Jupyter Notebook and import the required modules and class.

5. Load the model.

6. Perform a prediction for an individual by using the following values: **42, 2, 0, 0, 1, 2, 1, 0, 5, 8, 380, 1, −1, 0**.

   Expected output:

   ```
   [0]
   ```

   > **NOTE**
   >
   > The solution for this activity can be found on page 253.

INTERACTING WITH A TRAINED MODEL

Once the model has been created and saved, it is time for the last step of building a comprehensive machine learning program: allowing easy interaction with the model. This step not only allows the model to be reused, but also introduces efficiency to the implementation of machine learning solutions by allowing you to perform classifications using just input data.

There are several ways to interact with a model, and the decision that's made between choosing one or the other depends on the nature of the user (the individuals that will be making use of the model on a regular basis). Machine learning projects can be accessed in different ways, some of which require the use of an API, an online or offline program (application), or a website.

Moreover, once the channel is defined based on the preference or expertise of the users, it is important to code the connection between the final user and the model, which could be either a function or a class that deserializes the model and loads it, then performs the classification, and ultimately returns an output that is displayed again to the user.

The following diagram displays the relationship built between the channel and the model, where the icon to the left represents the model, the one in the middle is the function or class (the intermediary) performing the connection, and the icon to the right is the channel. Here, as we explained previously, the channel feeds the input data to the intermediary, which then feeds the information into the model to perform a classification. The output from the classification is sent back to the intermediary, which passes it along the channel in order to be displayed:

Figure 6.7: Illustration of the interaction between the user and the model

EXERCISE 6.03: CREATING A CLASS AND A CHANNEL TO INTERACT WITH A TRAINED MODEL

In this exercise, we will create a class in a text editor that takes the input data and feeds it to the model that was trained in *Exercise 6.01*, *Saving a Trained Model*, with the **Fertility Diagnosis** dataset. Additionally, we will create a form in a Jupyter Notebook, where users can input the data and obtain a prediction.

To create a class in a text editor, follow these steps:

1. Open a text editor of preference, such as PyCharm.

2. Import **pickle** and **os**:

    ```
    import pickle
    import os
    ```

3. Create a class object and name it **NN_Model**:

    ```
    Class NN_Model(object):
    ```

4. Inside of the class, create an initializer method that loads the file containing the saved model (**model_exercise.pkl**) into the code:

    ```
    def __init__(self):
        path = os.getcwd() + "/model_exercise.pkl"
        file = open(path, "rb")
        self.model = pickle.load(file)
    ```

    > **NOTE**
    >
    > Remember to indent the method inside of the class object.

    As a general rule, all the methods inside a class object must have the **self** argument. On the other hand, when defining the variable of the model using the **self** statement, it is possible to make use of the variable in any other method of the same class.

5. Inside the class named **NN_Model**, create a **predict** method. It should take in the feature values and input them as arguments to the **predict** method of the model so that it can feed them into the model and make a prediction:

```
def predict(self, season, age, childish, trauma, \
            surgical, fevers, alcohol, smoking, sitting):
    X = [[season, age, childish, trauma, surgical, \
         fevers, alcohol, smoking, sitting]]
    return self.model.predict(X)
```

> **NOTE**
>
> Remember to indent the method inside of the class object.

6. Save the code as a Python file (**.py**) and name it **exerciseClass.py**. The name of this file will be used to load the class into the Jupyter Notebook for the following steps.

   Now, let's code the frontend solution of the program, which includes creating a form where users can input data and obtain a prediction.

> **NOTE**
>
> For learning purposes, the form will be created in a Jupyter Notebook. However, it is often the case that the frontend is in the form of a website, an app, or something similar.

7. Open a Jupyter Notebook.

8. To import the model class that was saved as a Python file in *Step 6*, use the following code snippet:

```
from exerciseClass import NN_Model
```

9. Initialize the **NN_Model** class and store it in a variable called **model**:

```
model = NN_Model()
```

By making a call to the class that was saved in the Python file, the initializer method is automatically triggered, which loads the saved model into the variable.

10. Create a set of variables where the user can input the value for each feature, which will then be fed to the model. Use the following values:

> **NOTE**
>
> The # symbol in the code snippet below denotes a code comment. Comments are added into code to help explain specific bits of logic.

```
a = 1        # season in which the analysis was performed
b = 0.56     # age at the time of the analysis
c = 1        # childish disease
d = 1        # accident or serious trauma
e = 1        # surgical intervention
f = 0        # high fevers in the last year
g = 1        # frequency of alcohol consumption
h = -1       # smoking habit
i = 0.63     # number of hours spent sitting per day
```

11. Perform a prediction by using the **predict** method over the **model** variable. Input the feature values as arguments, taking into account that you must name them in the same way that you did when creating the **predict** function in the text editor:

```
pred = model.predict(season=a, age=b, childish=c, \
                     trauma=d, surgical=e, fevers=f, \
                     alcohol=g, smoking=h, sitting=i)
print(pred)
```

12. By printing the prediction, we get the following output:

```
['N']
```

CXY25

This means that the individual has a normal diagnosis.

> **NOTE**
>
> To access the source code for this specific section, please refer to
> https://packt.live/2MZPjg0.
>
> You can also run this example online at https://packt.live/3e4tQOC.
> You must execute the entire Notebook in order to get the desired result.

You have successfully created a function and a channel to interact with your model.

ACTIVITY 6.03: ALLOWING INTERACTION WITH THE BANK MARKETING DATASET MODEL

Consider the following scenario: after seeing the results that you presented in the previous activity, your boss has asked you to build a very simple way for him to test the model with data that he will receive over the course of the next month. If all the tests work well, he will be asking you to launch the program in a more effective way. Hence, you have decided to share a Jupyter Notebook with your boss, where he can just input the information and get a prediction.

> **NOTE**
>
> The following activity will be developed in two parts. The first part will involve building the class that connects the channel and the model, which will be developed using a text editor. The second part will be the creation of the channel, which will be done in a Jupyter Notebook.

Follow these steps to complete this activity:

1. In a text editor, create a class object that contains two main methods. One should be an initializer that loads the saved model, while the other should be a `predict` method, wherein the data is fed to the model to retrieve an output.

2. In a Jupyter Notebook, import and initialize the class that you created in the previous step. Next, create the variables that will hold the values for all the features of a new observation. Use the following values: **42, 2, 0, 0, 1, 2, 1, 0, 5, 8, 380, 1, −1, 0**.

3. Perform a prediction by applying the `predict` method.

Expected output: You will get **0** as the output when you complete this activity.

> **NOTE**
>
> The solution for this activity can be found on page 254.

SUMMARY

This chapter wraps up all of the concepts and techniques that are required to successfully train a machine learning model based on training data. In this chapter, we introduced the idea of building a comprehensive machine learning program that not only accounts for the stages involved in the preparation of the dataset and creation of the ideal model, but also the stage related to making the model accessible for future use, which is accomplished by carrying out three main processes: saving the model, loading the model, and creating a channel that allows users to easily interact with the model and obtain an outcome.

For saving and loading a model, the `pickle` module was introduced. This module is capable of serializing the model to save it in a file, while also being capable of deserializing it to make use of the model in the future.

Furthermore, to make the model accessible to users, the ideal channel (for example, an API, an application, a website, or a form) needs to be selected according to the type of user that will interact with the model. Then, an intermediary needs to be programmed that can connect the channel with the model. This intermediary is usually in the form of a function or a class.

The main objective of this book was to introduce scikit-learn's library as a way to develop machine learning solutions in a simple manner. After discussing the importance of and the different techniques involved in data exploration and pre-processing, this book divided its knowledge into the two main areas of machine learning, that is, supervised and unsupervised learning. The most common algorithms were discussed.

Finally, we explained the importance of measuring the performance of models by performing error analysis in order to improve the overall performance of the model on unseen data, and, ultimately, choosing the model that best represents the data. This final model should be saved so that you can use it in the future for visualizations or to perform predictions.

APPENDIX

CHAPTER 01: INTRODUCTION TO SCIKIT-LEARN

ACTIVITY 1.01: SELECTING A TARGET FEATURE AND CREATING A TARGET MATRIX

Solution:

1. Load the **titanic** dataset using the **seaborn** library:

```
import seaborn as sns
titanic = sns.load_dataset('titanic')
titanic.head(10)
```

The first couple of rows should look as follows:

	survived	pclass	sex	age	sibsp	parch	fare	embarked	class	who	adult_male	deck	embark_town	alive	alone
0	0	3	male	22.0	1	0	7.2500	S	Third	man	True	NaN	Southampton	no	False
1	1	1	female	38.0	1	0	71.2833	C	First	woman	False	C	Cherbourg	yes	False
2	1	3	female	26.0	0	0	7.9250	S	Third	woman	False	NaN	Southampton	yes	True
3	1	1	female	35.0	1	0	53.1000	S	First	woman	False	C	Southampton	yes	False
4	0	3	male	35.0	0	0	8.0500	S	Third	man	True	NaN	Southampton	no	True
5	0	3	male	NaN	0	0	8.4583	Q	Third	man	True	NaN	Queenstown	no	True
6	0	1	male	54.0	0	0	51.8625	S	First	man	True	E	Southampton	no	True
7	0	3	male	2.0	3	1	21.0750	S	Third	child	False	NaN	Southampton	no	False
8	1	3	female	27.0	0	2	11.1333	S	Third	woman	False	NaN	Southampton	yes	False
9	1	2	female	14.0	1	0	30.0708	C	Second	child	False	NaN	Cherbourg	yes	False

Figure 1.22: An image showing the first 10 instances of the Titanic dataset

2. Select your preferred target feature for the goal of this activity.

   The preferred target feature could be either **survived** or **alive**. This is mainly because both of them label whether a person survived the crash. For the following steps, the variable that's been chosen is **survived**. However, choosing **alive** will not affect the final shape of the variables.

3. Create both the features matrix and the target matrix. Make sure that you store the data from the features matrix in a variable, X, and the data from the target matrix in another variable, Y:

```
X = titanic.drop('survived',axis = 1)
Y = titanic['survived']
```

4. Print out the shape of **X**, as follows:

```
X.shape
```

The output is as follows:

```
(891, 14)
```

Do the same for **Y**:

```
Y.shape
```

The output is as follows:

```
(891,)
```

> **NOTE**
>
> To access the source code for this specific section, please refer to
> https://packt.live/37BwgSv.
>
> You can also run this example online at https://packt.live/2MXFtuP. **You must
> execute the entire Notebook in order to get the desired result.**

You have successfully split the dataset into two subsets, which will be used later on to train a model.

ACTIVITY 1.02: PRE-PROCESSING AN ENTIRE DATASET

Solution:

1. Import **seaborn** and the **LabelEncoder** class from scikit-learn. Next, load the **titanic** dataset and create the features matrix, including the following features: **sex**, **age**, **fare**, **class**, **embark_town**, and **alone**:

```
import seaborn as sns
from sklearn.preprocessing import LabelEncoder
titanic = sns.load_dataset('titanic')
X = titanic[['sex','age','fare','class',\
            'embark_town','alone']].copy()
X.shape
```

The features matrix was created as copies of the dataset in order to avoid getting a warning message every time the matrix was to be updated through the preprocessing process.

The output is as follows:

```
(891, 6)
```

2. Check for missing values in all the features. As we did previously, use **isnull()** to determine whether a value is missing and use **sum()** to sum up the occurrences of missing values along each feature:

```
print("Sex: " + str(X['sex'].isnull().sum()))
print("Age: " + str(X['age'].isnull().sum()))
print("Fare: " + str(X['fare'].isnull().sum()))
print("Class: " + str(X['class'].isnull().sum()))
print("Embark town: " + str(X['embark_town'].isnull().sum()))
print("Alone: " + str(X['alone'].isnull().sum()))
```

The output will look as follows:

```
Sex: 0
Age: 177
Fare: 0
Class: 0
Embark town: 2
Alone: 0
```

As you can see from the preceding output, only one feature contains a significant amount of missing values: **age**. As it contains many missing values that account for almost 20% of the total, the values should be replaced. The mean imputation methodology will be applied, as shown in the following code:

```
mean = X['age'].mean()
mean =round(mean)
X['age'].fillna(mean,inplace = True)
```

Next, discover the outliers present in the numeric features. Let's use three standard deviations as the measure to calculate the min and max threshold for numeric features:

```
features = ["age", "fare"]
for feature in features:
    min_ = X[feature].mean() - (3 * X[feature].std())
    max_ = X[feature].mean() + (3 * X[feature].std())
    X = X[X[feature] <= max_]
    X = X[X[feature] >= min_]
    print(feature,    ":", X.shape)
```

The output is as follows:

```
age: (884, 6)
fare: (864, 6)
```

The total count of outliers for the age and fare features is 7 and 20, respectively, reducing the shape of the initial matrix by 27 instances.

Next, using a **for** loop, discover outliers present in text features. The **value_counts()** function is used to count the occurrence of the classes in each feature:

```
features = ["sex", "class", "embark_town", "alone"]
for feature in features:
    count_ = X[feature].value_counts()
    print(feature)
    print(count_, "\n")
```

The output is as follows:

```
sex
male      562
female    302
Name: sex, dtype: int64

class
Third     489
First     192
Second    183
Name: class, dtype: int64

embark_town
Southampton    632
Cherbourg      154
Queenstown      76
Name: embark_town, dtype: int64

alone
True     524
False    340
Name: alone, dtype: int64
```

Figure 1.23: Count of occurrence of the classes in each feature

None of the classes for any of the features are considered to be outliers as they all represent over 5% of the entire dataset.

3. Convert all text features into their numeric representations. Use scikit-learn's **LabelEncoder** class, as shown in the following code:

```
enc = LabelEncoder()
X["sex"] = enc.fit_transform(X['sex'].astype('str'))
X["class"] = enc.fit_transform(X['class'].astype('str'))
X["embark_town"] = enc.fit_transform(X['embark_town'].\
                               astype('str'))
X["alone"] = enc.fit_transform(X['alone'].astype('str'))
```

Print out the top five instances of the features matrix to view the result of the conversion:

```
X.head()
```

The output is as follows:

	sex	age	fare	class	embark_town	alone
0	1	22.0	7.2500	2	2	0
1	0	38.0	71.2833	0	0	0
2	0	26.0	7.9250	2	2	1
3	0	35.0	53.1000	0	2	0
4	1	35.0	8.0500	2	2	1

Figure 1.24: A screenshot displaying the first five instances of the features matrix

4. Rescale your data, either by normalizing or standardizing it.

As you can see from the following code, all features go through the normalization process, but only those that don't meet the criteria of a normalized variable are changed:

```
X = (X - X.min()) / (X.max() - X.min())
X.head(10)
```

The top 10 rows of the final output are shown in the following screenshot:

	sex	age	fare	class	embark_town	alone
0	1.0	0.329064	0.043975	1.0	0.666667	0.0
1	0.0	0.573041	0.432369	0.0	0.000000	0.0
2	0.0	0.390058	0.048069	1.0	0.666667	1.0
3	0.0	0.527295	0.322078	0.0	0.666667	0.0
4	1.0	0.527295	0.048827	1.0	0.666667	1.0
5	1.0	0.451052	0.051304	1.0	0.333333	1.0
6	1.0	0.817017	0.314572	0.0	0.666667	1.0
7	1.0	0.024093	0.127831	1.0	0.666667	0.0
8	0.0	0.405306	0.067529	1.0	0.666667	0.0
9	0.0	0.207075	0.182395	0.5	0.000000	0.0

Figure 1.25: Displaying the first 10 instances of the normalized dataset

NOTE

To access the source code for this specific section, please refer to https://packt.live/2MY1wld.

You can also run this example online at https://packt.live/3e2lyqt.
You must execute the entire Notebook in order to get the desired result.

You have successfully performed data preprocessing over a dataset, which can now be used to train a ML algorithm.

CHAPTER 02: UNSUPERVISED LEARNING – REAL-LIFE APPLICATIONS

ACTIVITY 2.01: USING DATA VISUALIZATION TO AID THE PRE-PROCESSING PROCESS

Solution:

1. Import all the required elements to load the dataset and pre-process it:

    ```
    import pandas as pd
    import matplotlib.pyplot as plt
    import numpy as np
    ```

2. Load the previously downloaded dataset by using pandas' **read_csv()** function. Store the dataset in a pandas DataFrame named **data**:

    ```
    data = pd.read_csv("wholesale_customers_data.csv")
    ```

3. Check for missing values in your DataFrame. Using the **isnull()** function plus the **sum()** function, count the missing values of the entire dataset at once:

    ```
    data.isnull().sum()
    ```

    The output is as follows:

    ```
    Channel             0
    Region              0
    Fresh               0
    Milk                0
    Grocery             0
    Frozen              0
    Detergents_Paper    0
    Delicassen          0
    dtype: int64
    ```

    As you can see from the preceding screenshot, there are no missing values in the dataset.

4. Check for outliers in your DataFrame. Mark as outliers all the values that are three standard deviations away from the mean.

    The following code snippet allows you to look for outliers in the entire set of features at once. However, another valid method would be to check for outliers one feature at a time:

    ```
    outliers = {}
    ```

```
for i in range(data.shape[1]):
    min_t = data[data.columns[i]].mean() \
            - (3 * data[data.columns[i]].std())
    max_t = data[data.columns[i]].mean() \
            + (3 * data[data.columns[i]].std())
    count = 0
    for j in data[data.columns[i]]:
        if j < min_t or j > max_t:
            count += 1
    outliers[data.columns[i]] = [count,data.shape[0]-count]
```

```
print(outliers)
```

The count of outliers for each of the features is as follows:

```
{'Channel': [0, 440], 'Region': [0, 440], 'Fresh': [7, 433], 'Milk':
[9, 431], 'Grocery': [7, 433], 'Frozen': [6, 434], 'Detergents_
Paper': [10, 430], 'Delicassen': [4, 436]}
```

As you can see from the preceding screenshot, some features do have outliers. Considering that there are only a few outliers for each feature, there are two possible ways to handle them.

First, you could decide to delete the outliers. This decision can be supported by displaying a histogram for the features with outliers:

```
plt.hist(data["Fresh"])
plt.show()
```

The output is as follows:

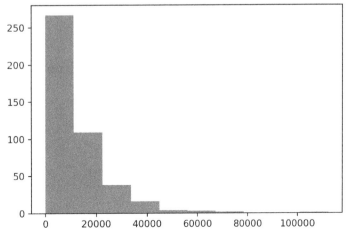

Figure 2.14: An example histogram plot for the "Fresh" feature

In the preceding plot, the *x-axis* represents the values present in the dataset for the selected feature, while the y-axis refers to the number of occurrences of each value. It is worth mentioning that histograms built for continuous values make ranges out of the values in order to be able to count their occurrences in the dataset.

For instance, for the feature named **Fresh**, it can be seen through the histogram that most instances are represented by values below 40,000. Hence, deleting the instances above that value will not affect the performance of the model.

On the other hand, the second approach would be to leave the outliers as they are, considering that they do not represent a large portion of the dataset, which can be supported with data visualization tools using a pie chart. Refer to the code and the output that follows:

```
plt.figure(figsize=(8,8))
plt.pie(outliers["Detergents_Paper"],autopct="%.2f")
plt.show()
```

The output is as follows:

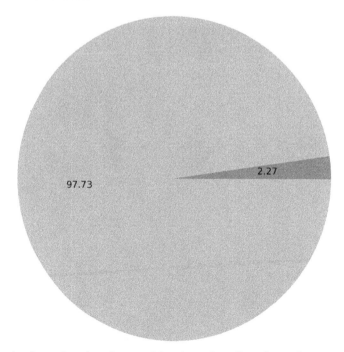

Figure 2.15: A pie chart showing the participation of outliers from the Detergents_papers feature in the dataset

The preceding diagram shows the participation of the outliers from the **Detergents_papers** feature, which was the feature with the most outliers in the dataset. Only 2.27% of the values are outliers, a value so low that it will not affect the performance of the model either.

For the solution in this book, it was decided to keep the outliers since they are not likely to affect the performance of the model.

5. Rescale the data.

For this solution, the formula for standardization has been used. Note that the formula can be applied to the entire dataset at once, instead of being applied individually to each feature:

```
data_standardized = (data - data.mean())/data.std()
data_standardized.head()
```

The output is as follows:

	Channel	Region	Fresh	Milk	Grocery	Frozen	Detergents_Paper	Delicassen
0	1.447005	0.589997	0.052873	0.522972	-0.041068	-0.588697	-0.043519	-0.066264
1	1.447005	0.589997	-0.390857	0.543839	0.170125	-0.269829	0.086309	0.089050
2	1.447005	0.589997	-0.446521	0.408073	-0.028125	-0.137379	0.133080	2.240742
3	-0.689512	0.589997	0.099998	-0.623310	-0.392530	0.686363	-0.498021	0.093305
4	1.447005	0.589997	0.839284	-0.052337	-0.079266	0.173661	-0.231654	1.297870

Figure 2.16: Rescaled data

> **NOTE**
>
> To access the source code for this specific section, please refer to https://packt.live/2Y3ooGh.
>
> You can also run this example online at https://packt.live/2B8vKPI.
> You must execute the entire Notebook in order to get the desired result.

You have successfully pre-processed the Wholesale Customers dataset, which will be used in subsequent activities to build a model that will classify these observations into clusters.

ACTIVITY 2.02: APPLYING THE K-MEANS ALGORITHM TO A DATASET

Solution:

1. Open the Jupyter Notebook that you used for the previous activity. There, you should have imported all the required libraries and performed the necessary steps to pre-process the dataset.

   The standardized data should look as follows:

	Channel	Region	Fresh	Milk	Grocery	Frozen	Detergents_Paper	Delicassen
0	1.447005	0.589997	0.052873	0.522972	-0.041068	-0.588697	-0.043519	-0.066264
1	1.447005	0.589997	-0.390857	0.543839	0.170125	-0.269829	0.086309	0.089050
2	1.447005	0.589997	-0.446521	0.408073	-0.028125	-0.137379	0.133080	2.240742
3	-0.689512	0.589997	0.099998	-0.623310	-0.392530	0.686363	-0.498021	0.093305
4	1.447005	0.589997	0.839284	-0.052337	-0.079266	0.173661	-0.231654	1.297870

   Figure 2.17: A screenshot displaying the first five instances of the standardized dataset

2. Calculate the average distance of data points from its centroid in relation to the number of clusters. Based on this distance, select the appropriate number of clusters to train the model on.

   First, import the algorithm class:

   ```
   from sklearn.cluster import KMeans
   ```

   Next, using the code in the following snippet, calculate the average distance of data points from its centroid based on the number of clusters created:

   ```
   ideal_k = []
   for i in range(1,21):
       est_kmeans = KMeans(n_clusters=i, random_state=0)
       est_kmeans.fit(data_standardized)
       ideal_k.append([i,est_kmeans.inertia_])


   ideal_k = np.array(ideal_k)
   ```

   Finally, plot the relation to find the breaking point of the line and select the number of clusters:

   ```
   plt.plot(ideal_k[:,0],ideal_k[:,1])
   plt.show()
   ```

The output is as follows:

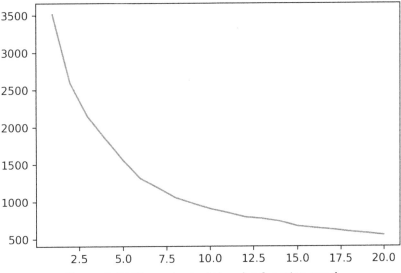

Figure 2.18: The output of the plot function used

Again, the *x-axis* represents the number of clusters, while the *y-axis* refers to the calculated average distance of the data points in a cluster from their centroid.

3. Train the model and assign a cluster to each data point in your dataset. Plot the results.

To train the model, use the following code:

```
est_kmeans = KMeans(n_clusters=6, random_state = 0)
est_kmeans.fit(data_standardized)
pred_kmeans = est_kmeans.predict(data_standardized)
```

The number of clusters selected is **6**; however, since there is no exact breaking point, values between 5 and 10 are also acceptable.

Finally, plot the results of the clustering process. Since the dataset contains eight different features, choose two features to draw at once, as shown in the following code:

```
plt.subplots(1, 2, sharex='col', \
            sharey='row', figsize=(16,8))
plt.scatter(data.iloc[:,5], data.iloc[:,3], \
            c=pred_kmeans, s=20)
```

```
plt.xlim([0, 20000])
plt.ylim([0, 20000])
plt.xlabel('Frozen')
plt.subplot(1, 2, 1)
plt.scatter(data.iloc[:,4], data.iloc[:,3], \
            c=pred_kmeans, s=20)
plt.xlim([0, 20000])
plt.ylim([0,20000])
plt.xlabel('Grocery')
plt.ylabel('Milk')
plt.show()
```

The output is as follows:

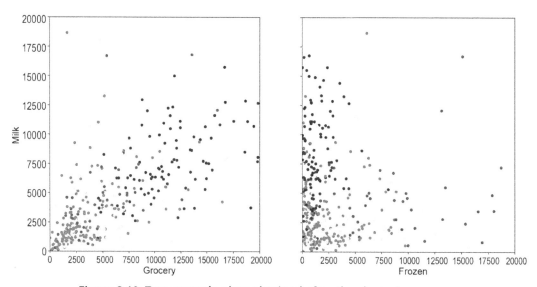

Figure 2.19: Two example plots obtained after the clustering process

NOTE

To access the source code for this activity, please refer to
https://packt.live/3fhgO0y.

You can also run this example online at https://packt.live/3eeEOB6.
You must execute the entire Notebook in order to get the desired result.

The **subplots()** function from **matplotlib** has been used to plot two scatter graphs at a time. For each graph, the axes represent the values for a selected feature in relation to the values of another feature. As can be seen from the plots, there is no obvious visual relation due to the fact that we are only able to use two of the eight features present in the dataset. However, the final output of the model creates six different clusters that represent six different profiles of clients.

ACTIVITY 2.03: APPLYING THE MEAN-SHIFT ALGORITHM TO A DATASET

Solution:

1. Open the Jupyter Notebook that you used for the previous activity.

2. Train the model and assign a cluster to each data point in your dataset. Plot the results.

   First, import the algorithm class:

   ```
   from sklearn.cluster import MeanShift
   ```

   To train the model, use the following code:

   ```
   est_meanshift = MeanShift(0.4)
   est_meanshift.fit(data_standardized)
   pred_meanshift = est_meanshift.predict(data_standardized)
   ```

   The model was trained using a bandwidth of **0.4**. However, feel free to test other values to see how the result changes.

   Finally, plot the results of the clustering process. As the dataset contains eight different features, choose two features to draw at once, as shown in the following snippet. Similar to the previous activity, the separation between clusters is not seen visually due to the capability to only draw two out of the eight features:

   ```
   plt.subplots(1, 2, sharex='col', \
                sharey='row', figsize=(16,8))
   plt.scatter(data.iloc[:,5], data.iloc[:,3], \
               c=pred_meanshift, s=20)
   plt.xlim([0, 20000])
   plt.ylim([0,20000])
   ```

```
plt.xlabel('Frozen')
plt.subplot(1, 2, 1)
plt.scatter(data.iloc[:,4], data.iloc[:,3], \
            c=pred_meanshift, s=20)
plt.xlim([0, 20000])
plt.ylim([0,20000])
plt.xlabel('Grocery')
plt.ylabel('Milk')
plt.show()
```

The output is as follows:

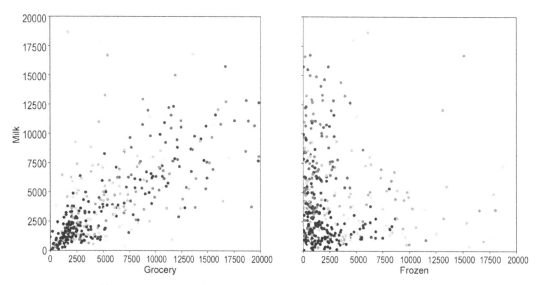

Figure 2.20: Example plots obtained at the end of the process

For each of the plots, the axes represent the values of a selected feature, against the values of another feature.

> **NOTE**
>
> To access the source code for this activity, please refer to
> https://packt.live/3fviVy1.
>
> You can also run this example online at https://packt.live/2Y1aqEF.
> You must execute the entire Notebook in order to get the desired result.

You have successfully applied the mean-shift algorithm over the Wholesale Customers dataset. Later on, you will be able to compare the results of the different algorithms over the same dataset to choose the one that performs the best.

ACTIVITY 2.04: APPLYING THE DBSCAN ALGORITHM TO THE DATASET

Solution:

1. Open the Jupyter Notebook that you used for the previous activity.

2. Train the model and assign a cluster to each data point in your dataset. Plot the results.

    First, import the algorithm class:

    ```
    from sklearn.cluster import DBSCAN
    ```

    To train the model, use the following code:

    ```
    est_dbscan = DBSCAN(eps=0.8)
    pred_dbscan = est_dbscan.fit_predict(data_standardized)
    ```

    The model was trained using an epsilon value of **0.8**. However, feel free to test other values to see how the results change.

    Finally, plot the results of the clustering process. As the dataset contains eight different features, choose two features to draw at once, as shown in the following code:

    ```
    plt.subplots(1, 2, sharex='col', \
                 sharey='row', figsize=(16,8))
    plt.scatter(data.iloc[:,5], data.iloc[:,3], \
                c=pred_dbscan, s=20)
    plt.xlim([0, 20000])
    plt.ylim([0,20000])
    plt.xlabel('Frozen')
    plt.subplot(1, 2, 1)
    plt.scatter(data.iloc[:,4], data.iloc[:,3], \
                c=pred_dbscan, s=20)
    plt.xlim([0, 20000])
    plt.ylim([0,20000])
    plt.xlabel('Grocery')
    plt.ylabel('Milk')
    plt.show()
    ```

The output is as follows:

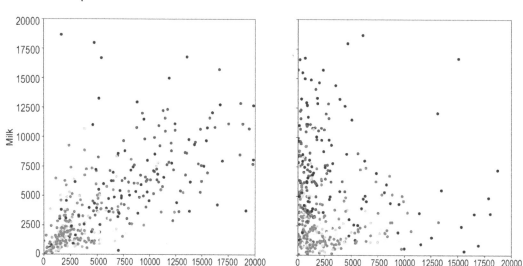

Figure 2.21: Example plots obtained at the end of the clustering process

> **NOTE**
>
> To access the source code for this activity, please refer to
> https://packt.live/2YCFvh8.
>
> You can also run this example online at https://packt.live/2MZgnvC. You must
> execute the entire Notebook in order to get the desired result.

Similar to the previous activity, the separation between clusters is not seen visually due to the capability to only draw two out of the eight features at once.

ACTIVITY 2.05: MEASURING AND COMPARING THE PERFORMANCE OF THE ALGORITHMS

Solution:

1. Open the Jupyter Notebook that you used for the previous activity.

2. Calculate both the Silhouette Coefficient score and the Calinski–Harabasz index for all the models that you trained previously.

   First, import the metrics:

   ```
   from sklearn.metrics import silhouette_score
   from sklearn.metrics import calinski_harabasz_score
   ```

Calculate the Silhouette Coefficient score for all the algorithms, as shown in the following code:

```
kmeans_score = silhouette_score(data_standardized, \
                                pred_kmeans, \
                                metric='euclidean')
meanshift_score = silhouette_score(data_standardized, \
                                   pred_meanshift, \
                                   metric='euclidean')
dbscan_score = silhouette_score(data_standardized, \
                                pred_dbscan, \
                                metric='euclidean')
print(kmeans_score, meanshift_score, dbscan_score)
```

The scores come to be around **0.3515**, **0.0933**, and **0.1685** for the k-means, mean-shift, and DBSCAN algorithms, respectively.

Finally, calculate the Calinski–Harabasz index for all the algorithms. The following is a snippet of the code for this:

```
kmeans_score = calinski_harabasz_score(data_standardized, \
                                       pred_kmeans)
meanshift_score = calinski_harabasz_score(data_standardized, \
                                          pred_meanshift)
dbscan_score = calinski_harabasz_score(data_standardized, \
                                       pred_dbscan)
print(kmeans_score, meanshift_score, dbscan_score)
```

The scores come to be approximately **145.73**, **112.90**, and **42.45** for the three algorithms in the order given in the preceding code snippet.

> **NOTE**
>
> To access the source code for this activity, please refer to https://packt.live/2Y2xHWR.
>
> You can also run this example online at https://packt.live/3hszegy. You must execute the entire Notebook in order to get the desired result.

By quickly looking at the results we obtained for both metrics, it is possible to conclude that the k-means algorithm outperforms the other models, and hence should be the one that's selected to solve the data problem.

CHAPTER 03: SUPERVISED LEARNING – KEY STEPS

ACTIVITY 3.01: DATA PARTITIONING ON A HANDWRITTEN DIGIT DATASET

Solution:

1. Import all the required elements to split a dataset, as well as the **load_digits** function from scikit-learn to load the **digits** dataset. Use the following code to do so:

```
from sklearn.datasets import load_digits
import pandas as pd
from sklearn.model_selection import train_test_split
from sklearn.model_selection import KFold
```

2. Load the **digits** dataset and create Pandas DataFrames containing the features and target matrices:

```
digits = load_digits()
X = pd.DataFrame(digits.data)
Y = pd.DataFrame(digits.target)
print(X.shape, Y.shape)
```

The shape of your features and target matrices should be as follows, respectively:

```
(1797, 64) (1797, 1)
```

3. Perform the conventional split approach, using a split ratio of 60/20/20%.

Using the **train_test_split** function, split the data into an initial train set and a test set:

```
X_new, X_test, \
Y_new, Y_test = train_test_split(X, Y, test_size=0.2)
print(X_new.shape, Y_new.shape, X_test.shape, Y_test.shape)
```

The shape of the sets that you created should be as follows:

```
(1437, 64) (1437, 1) (360, 64) (360, 1)
```

Next, calculate the value of **test_size**, which sets the size of the dev set equal to the size of the test set that was created previously:

```
dev_size = X_test.shape[0]/X_new.shape[0]
print(dev_size)
```

The result of the preceding operation is **0.2505**.

Finally, split **X_new** and **Y_new** into the final train and dev sets. Use the following code to do so:

```
X_train, X_dev, \
Y_train, Y_dev = train_test_split(X_new, Y_new, \
                                  test_size = dev_size)


print(X_train.shape, Y_train.shape, X_dev.shape, \
      Y_dev.shape, X_test.shape, Y_test.shape)
```

The output from the preceding snippet is as follows:

```
(1077, 64) (1077, 1) (360, 64) (360, 1) (360, 64) (360, 1)
```

4. Using the same DataFrames, perform a 10-fold cross-validation split.

   First, divide the datasets into initial training and testing sets:

```
X_new_2, X_test_2, \
Y_new_2, Y_test_2 = train_test_split(X, Y, test_size=0.1)
```

Using the **KFold** class, perform a 10-fold split:

```
kf = KFold(n_splits = 10)
splits = kf.split(X_new_2)
```

Remember that cross-validation performs a different configuration of splits, shuffling data each time. Considering this, perform a **for** loop that will go through all the split configurations:

```
for train_index, dev_index in splits:
    X_train_2, X_dev_2 = X_new_2.iloc[train_index,:], \
                         X_new_2.iloc[dev_index,:]
    Y_train_2, Y_dev_2 = Y_new_2.iloc[train_index,:], \
                         Y_new_2.iloc[dev_index,:]
```

The code in charge of training and evaluating the model should be inside the body of the **for** loop in order to train and evaluate the model with each configuration of splits:

```
print(X_train_2.shape, Y_train_2.shape, X_dev_2.shape, \
      Y_dev_2.shape, X_test_2.shape, Y_test_2.shape)
```

By printing the shape of all the subsets, as per the preceding snippet, the output is as follows:

```
(1456, 64) (1456, 1) (161, 64) (161, 1) (180, 64) (180, 1)
```

> **NOTE**
>
> To access the source code for this specific section, please refer to https://packt.live/37xatv3.
>
> You can also run this example online at https://packt.live/2Y2noIS. You must execute the entire Notebook in order to get the desired result.

You have successfully split a dataset using both the conventional split approach, as well as the cross-validation one. These sets can now be used to train outstanding models that perform well on unseen data.

ACTIVITY 3.02: EVALUATING THE PERFORMANCE OF THE MODEL TRAINED ON A HANDWRITTEN DATASET

Solution:

1. Import all the required elements to load and split a dataset in order to train a model and evaluate the performance of the classification tasks:

```
from sklearn.datasets import load_digits
import pandas as pd
from sklearn.model_selection import train_test_split
from sklearn import tree
from sklearn.metrics import confusion_matrix
from sklearn.metrics import accuracy_score
from sklearn.metrics import precision_score
from sklearn.metrics import recall_score
```

2. Load the **digits** toy dataset from scikit-learn and create Pandas DataFrames containing the features and target matrices:

```
digits = load_digits()
X = pd.DataFrame(digits.data)
Y = pd.DataFrame(digits.target)
```

3. Split the data into training and testing sets. Use 20% as the size of the testing set:

```
X_train, X_test, \
Y_train, Y_test = train_test_split(X,Y, test_size = 0.2,\
                                    random_state = 0)
```

4. Train a decision tree on the train set. Then, use the model to predict the class label on the test set (hint: to train the decision tree, revisit *Exercise 3.04, Calculating Different Evaluation Metrics on a Classification Task*):

```
model = tree.DecisionTreeClassifier(random_state = 0)
model = model.fit(X_train, Y_train)
Y_pred = model.predict(X_test)
```

5. Use scikit-learn to construct a confusion matrix:

```
confusion_matrix(Y_test, Y_pred)
```

The output of the confusion matrix is as follows:

```
array([[24,  0,  0,  0,  0,  0,  1,  0,  0,  2],
       [ 0, 31,  0,  2,  1,  0,  1,  0,  0,  0],
       [ 1,  0, 29,  0,  0,  0,  2,  2,  1,  1],
       [ 0,  0,  2, 27,  0,  0,  0,  0,  0,  0],
       [ 1,  1,  0,  0, 26,  0,  1,  1,  0,  0],
       [ 0,  1,  1,  0,  0, 34,  0,  0,  1,  3],
       [ 1,  1,  1,  1,  1,  0, 39,  0,  0,  0],
       [ 0,  0,  0,  0,  0,  1,  1, 37,  0,  0],
       [ 1,  3,  3,  5,  0,  1,  0,  1, 24,  1],
       [ 0,  0,  1,  4,  0,  1,  0,  0,  1, 34]])
```

Figure 3.14: Output of the confusion matrix

6. Calculate the accuracy of the model:

```
accuracy = accuracy_score(Y_test, Y_pred)
print("accuracy:", accuracy)
```

The accuracy is equal to **84.72%**.

7. Calculate the precision and recall. Considering that both the precision and recall can only be calculated on binary data, we'll assume that we are only interested in classifying instances as number 6 or any other number:

```
Y_test_2 = Y_test[:]
Y_test_2[Y_test_2 != 6] = 1
Y_test_2[Y_test_2 == 6] = 0
Y_pred_2 = Y_pred
Y_pred_2[Y_pred_2 != 6] = 1
Y_pred_2[Y_pred_2 == 6] = 0

precision = precision_score(Y_test_2, Y_pred_2)
print("precision:", precision)

recall = recall_score(Y_test_2, Y_pred_2)
print("recall:", recall)
```

The output from the preceding code snippet is as follows:

```
precision: 0.9841269841269841
recall: 0.9810126582278481
```

According to this, the precision and recall scores should be equal to **98.41**% and **98.10**%, respectively.

> **NOTE**
>
> To access the source code for this specific section, please refer to https://packt.live/2UJMFPC.
>
> You can also run this example online at https://packt.live/2zwqkgX.
> You must execute the entire Notebook in order to get the desired result.

You have successfully measured the performance of classification tasks.

ACTIVITY 3.03: PERFORMING ERROR ANALYSIS ON A MODEL TRAINED TO RECOGNIZE HANDWRITTEN DIGITS

Solution:

1. Import the required elements to load and split a dataset. We will do this to train the model and measure its accuracy:

```
from sklearn.datasets import load_digits
import pandas as pd
from sklearn.model_selection import train_test_split
import numpy as np
from sklearn import tree
from sklearn.metrics import accuracy_score
```

2. Load the **digits** toy dataset from scikit-learn and create Pandas DataFrames containing the features and target matrices:

```
digits = load_digits()
X = pd.DataFrame(digits.data)
Y = pd.DataFrame(digits.target)
```

3. Split the data into training, validation, and testing sets. Use **0.1** as the size of the test set, and an equivalent number to build a validation set of the same shape:

```
X_new, X_test, \
Y_new, Y_test = train_test_split(X, Y, test_size = 0.1,\
                                 random_state = 101)

test_size = X_test.shape[0] / X_new.shape[0]

X_train, X_dev, \
Y_train, Y_dev = train_test_split(X_new, Y_new, \
                                  test_size= test_size, \
                                  random_state = 101)

print(X_train.shape, Y_train.shape, X_dev.shape, \
      Y_dev.shape, X_test.shape, Y_test.shape)
```

The resulting shapes are as follows:

```
(1437, 64) (1437, 1) (180, 64) (180, 1) (180, 64) (180, 1)
```

4. Create a train/dev set for both the features and the target values that contains **90** instances/labels of the train set and **90** instances/labels of the dev set:

```
np.random.seed(101)

indices_train = np.random.randint(0, len(X_train), 90)
indices_dev = np.random.randint(0, len(X_dev), 90)

X_train_dev = pd.concat([X_train.iloc[indices_train,:], \
                         X_dev.iloc[indices_dev,:]])
Y_train_dev = pd.concat([Y_train.iloc[indices_train,:], \
                         Y_dev.iloc[indices_dev,:]])

print(X_train_dev.shape, Y_train_dev.shape)
```

The resulting shapes are as follows:

```
(180, 64) (180, 1)
```

5. Train a decision tree on that training set data:

```
model = tree.DecisionTreeClassifier(random_state = 101)
model = model.fit(X_train, Y_train)
```

6. Calculate the error rate for all sets of data and determine which condition is affecting the performance of the model:

```
sets = ["Training", "Train/dev", "Validation", "Testing"]
X_sets = [X_train, X_train_dev, X_dev, X_test]
Y_sets = [Y_train, Y_train_dev, Y_dev, Y_test]

scores = {}
for i in range(0, len(X_sets)):
    pred = model.predict(X_sets[i])
    score = accuracy_score(Y_sets[i], pred)
    scores[sets[i]] = score

print(scores)
```

The output is as follows:

```
{'Training': 1.0, 'Train/dev': 0.9444444444444444, 'Validation':
0.8833333333333333, 'Testing': 0.8833333333333333}
```

The error rates can be seen in the following table:

Sets	Error Rate
Bayes error	0
Training set	0
Train/dev set	0.0556
Validation set	0.1167
Testing set	0.1167

Figure 3.15: Error rates of the Handwritten Digits model

From the preceding results, it can be concluded that the model is equally suffering from variance and data mismatch.

> **NOTE**
>
> To access the source code for this specific section, please refer to https://packt.live/3d0c4uM.
>
> You can also run this example online at https://packt.live/3eeFlTC.
> You must execute the entire Notebook in order to get the desired result.

You have now successfully performed an error analysis to determine a course of action to improve the model's performance.

CHAPTER 04: SUPERVISED LEARNING ALGORITHMS: PREDICTING ANNUAL INCOME

ACTIVITY 4.01: TRAINING A NAÏVE BAYES MODEL FOR OUR CENSUS INCOME DATASET

Solution:

1. In a Jupyter Notebook, import all the required elements to load and split the dataset, as well as to train a Naïve Bayes algorithm:

```
import pandas as pd
from sklearn.model_selection import train_test_split
from sklearn.naive_bayes import GaussianNB
```

2. Load the pre-processed Census Income dataset. Next, separate the features from the target by creating two variables, **X** and **Y**:

```
data = pd.read_csv("census_income_dataset_preprocessed.csv")
X = data.drop("target", axis=1)
Y = data["target"]
```

Note that there are several ways to achieve the separation of **X** and **Y**. Use the one that you feel most comfortable with. However, take into account that **X** should contain the features of all instances, while **Y** should contain the class labels of all instances.

3. Divide the dataset into training, validation, and testing sets, using a split ratio of 10%:

```
X_new, X_test, \
Y_new, Y_test = train_test_split(X, Y, test_size=0.1, \
                                 random_state=101)

test_size = X_test.shape[0] / X_new.shape[0]

X_train, X_dev, \
Y_train, Y_dev = train_test_split(X_new, Y_new, \
                                  test_size=test_size, \
                                  random_state=101)

print(X_train.shape, Y_train.shape, X_dev.shape, \
      Y_dev.shape, X_test.shape, Y_test.shape)
```

The final shape will look as follows:

```
(26047, 9) (26047,) (3257, 9) (3257,) (3257, 9) (3257,)
```

4. Use the **fit** method to train a Naïve Bayes model on the training sets (**X_train** and **Y_train**):

```
model_NB = GaussianNB()
model_NB.fit(X_train,Y_train)
```

5. Finally, perform a prediction using the model that you trained previously for a new instance with the following values for each feature – **39**, **6**, **13**, **4**, **0**, **2174**, **0**, **40**, **38**:

```
pred_1 = model_NB.predict([[39,6,13,4,0,2174,0,40,38]])
print(pred_1)
```

The output from the prediction is as follows:

```
[0]
```

> **NOTE**
>
> To access the source code for this specific section, please refer to https://packt.live/3ht1TCs.
>
> You can also run this example online at https://packt.live/2zwqxkf.
> You must execute the entire Notebook in order to get the desired result.

This means that the individual has an income less than or equal to 50K, considering that 0 is the label for individuals with a salary less than or equal to 50K.

ACTIVITY 4.02: TRAINING A DECISION TREE MODEL FOR OUR CENSUS INCOME DATASET

Solution:

1. Open the Jupyter Notebook that you used for the previous activity and import the decision tree algorithm from scikit-learn:

```
from sklearn.tree import DecisionTreeClassifier
```

2. Train the model using the **fit** method on the **DecisionTreeClassifier** class from scikit-learn. To train the model, use the training set data from the previous activity (**X_train** and **Y_train**):

```
model_tree = DecisionTreeClassifier(random_state=101)
model_tree.fit(X_train,Y_train)
```

3. Finally, perform a prediction using the model that you trained before for a new instance with the following values for each feature – **39**, **6**, **13**, **4**, **0**, **2174**, **0**, **40**, **38**:

```
pred_2 = model_tree.predict([[39,6,13,4,0,2174,0,40,38]])
print(pred_2)
```

The output from the preceding code snippet is as follows:

```
[0]
```

> **NOTE**
>
> To access the source code for this specific section, please refer to
> https://packt.live/2zxQIqV.
>
> You can also run this example online at https://packt.live/2AC7iWX.
> You must execute the entire Notebook in order to get the desired result.

This means that the subject has an income lower than or equal to 50K.

ACTIVITY 4.03: TRAINING AN SVM MODEL FOR OUR CENSUS INCOME DATASET

Solution:

1. Open the Jupyter Notebook that you used for the previous activity and import the SVM algorithm from scikit-learn:

```
from sklearn.svm import SVC
```

2. Train the model using the **fit** method on the **SVC** class from scikit-learn. To train the model, use the training set data from the previous activity (**X_train** and **Y_train**):

```
model_svm = SVC()
model_svm.fit(X_train, Y_train)
```

3. Finally, perform a prediction using the model that you trained before for a new instance with the following values for each feature – **39**, **6**, **13**, **4**, **0**, **2174**, **0**, **40**, **38**:

```
pred_3 = model_svm.predict([[39,6,13,4,0,2174,0,40,38]])
print(pred_3)
```

The output is as follows:

```
[0]
```

The prediction for the individual is equal to zero, which means that the individual has an income below or equal to **50K**.

> **NOTE**
>
> To access the source code for this specific section, please refer to https://packt.live/2Nb6J9z.
>
> You can also run this example online at https://packt.live/3hbpCGm.
> You must execute the entire Notebook in order to get the desired result.

CHAPTER 05: ARTIFICIAL NEURAL NETWORKS: PREDICTING ANNUAL INCOME

ACTIVITY 5.01: TRAINING AN MLP FOR OUR CENSUS INCOME DATASET

Solution:

1. Import all the elements required to load and split a dataset, to train an MLP, and to measure accuracy:

```
import pandas as pd
from sklearn.model_selection import train_test_split
from sklearn.neural_network import MLPClassifier
from sklearn.metrics import accuracy_score
```

2. Using the preprocessed Census Income Dataset, separate the features from the target, creating the variables **X** and **Y**:

```
data = pd.read_csv("census_income_dataset_preprocessed.csv")
X = data.drop("target", axis=1)
Y = data["target"]
```

As explained previously, there are several ways to achieve the separation of **X** and **Y**, and the main thing to consider is that **X** should contain the features for all instances, while **Y** should contain the class label of all instances.

3. Divide the dataset into training, validation, and testing sets, using a split ratio of 10%:

```
X_new, X_test, \
Y_new, Y_test = train_test_split(X, Y, test_size=0.1, \
                                 random_state=101)


test_size = X_test.shape[0] / X_new.shape[0]


X_train, X_dev, \
Y_train, Y_dev = train_test_split(X_new, Y_new, \
                                  test_size=test_size, \
                                  random_state=101)


print(X_train.shape, X_dev.shape, X_test.shape, \
      Y_train.shape, Y_dev.shape, Y_test.shape)
```

The shape of the sets created should be as follows:

```
(26047, 9) (3257, 9) (3257, 9) (26047,) (3257,) (3257,)
```

4. Instantiate the **MLPClassifier** class from scikit-learn and train the model with the training data. Leave the hyperparameters to their default values. Again, use a **random_state** equal to **101**:

```
model = MLPClassifier(random_state=101)
model = model.fit(X_train, Y_train)
```

5. Calculate the accuracy of the model for all three sets (training, validation, and testing):

```
sets = ["Training", "Validation", "Testing"]
X_sets = [X_train, X_dev, X_test]
Y_sets = [Y_train, Y_dev, Y_test]

accuracy = {}
for i in range(0,len(X_sets)):
    pred = model.predict(X_sets[i])
    score = accuracy_score(Y_sets[i], pred)
    accuracy[sets[i]] = score

print(accuracy)
```

The accuracy score for the three sets should be as follows:

```
{'Training': 0.8465909090909091, 'Validation': 0.8246314496314496,
'Testing': 0.8415719987718759}
```

> **NOTE**
>
> To access the source code for this specific section, please refer to https://packt.live/3hneWFr.
>
> This section does not currently have an online interactive example, and will need to be run locally.

You have successfully trained an MLP model to solve a real-life data problem.

ACTIVITY 5.02: COMPARING DIFFERENT MODELS TO CHOOSE THE BEST FIT FOR THE CENSUS INCOME DATA PROBLEM

Solution:

1. Open the Jupyter Notebooks that you used to train the models.

2. Compare the four models, based only on their accuracy scores.

    By taking the accuracy scores of the models from the previous chapter, and the accuracy of the model trained in this chapter, it is possible to perform a final comparison to choose the model that best solves the data problem. To do so, the following table displays the accuracy scores for all four models:

	Naïve Bayes	Decision Tree	SVM	Neural Network
Training sets	0.7971	0.9724	0.8025	0.8673
Validation sets	0.7902	0.8115	0.8115	0.8311
Testing sets	0.8084	0.8235	0.8235	0.8520

Figure 5.15: Accuracy scores of all four models for the Census Income Dataset

3. On the basis of the accuracy scores, identify the model that best solves the data problem.

    To identify the model that best solves the data problem, begin by comparing the accuracy rates over the training sets. From this, it is possible to conclude that the decision tree model is a better fit for the data problem. Nonetheless, the performance over the validation and testing sets is lower than the one achieved using the MLP, which is an indication of the presence of high variance in the decision tree model.

Hence, a good approach would be to address the high variance of the decision tree model by simplifying the model. This can be achieved by adding a pruning argument that "trims" the leaves of the tree to simplify it and ignore some of the details of the tree in order to generalize the model to the data. Ideally, the model should be able to reach a similar level of accuracy for all three sets, which would make it the best model for the data problem.

However, if the model is not able to overcome the high variance, and assuming that all the models have been fine-tuned to achieve the maximum performance possible, the MLP should be the model that is selected, considering that it performs best over the testing sets. This is mainly because the performance of the model over the testing set is the one that defines its overall performance over unseen data, which means that the one with higher testing-set performance will be more useful in the long term.

CHAPTER 06: BUILDING YOUR OWN PROGRAM

ACTIVITY 6.01: PERFORMING THE PREPARATION AND CREATION STAGES FOR THE BANK MARKETING DATASET

Solution:

> **NOTE**
>
> To ensure the reproducibility of the results available at https://packt.live/2RpIhn9, make sure that you use a **random_state** of 0 when splitting the datasets and a **random_state** of 2 when training the models.

1. Open a Jupyter Notebook and import all the required elements:

```
import pandas as pd
from sklearn.preprocessing import LabelEncoder
from sklearn.model_selection import train_test_split
from sklearn.tree import DecisionTreeClassifier
from sklearn.neural_network import MLPClassifier
from sklearn.metrics import precision_score
```

2. Load the dataset into the notebook. Make sure that you load the one that was edited previously, named **bank-full-dataset.csv**, which is also available at https://packt.live/2wnJyny:

```
data = pd.read_csv("bank-full-dataset.csv")
data.head(10)
```

The output is as follows:

	age	job	marital	education	default	balance	housing	loan	contact	day	month	duration	campaign	pdays	previous	poutcome	y
0	58	management	married	tertiary	no	2143	yes	no	NaN	5	may	261	1	-1	0	NaN	no
1	44	technician	single	secondary	no	29	yes	no	NaN	5	may	151	1	-1	0	NaN	no
2	33	entrepreneur	married	secondary	no	2	yes	yes	NaN	5	may	76	1	-1	0	NaN	no
3	47	blue-collar	married	NaN	no	1506	yes	no	NaN	5	may	92	1	-1	0	NaN	no
4	33	NaN	single	NaN	no	1	no	no	NaN	5	may	198	1	-1	0	NaN	no
5	35	management	married	tertiary	no	231	yes	no	NaN	5	may	139	1	-1	0	NaN	no
6	28	management	single	tertiary	no	447	yes	yes	NaN	5	may	217	1	-1	0	NaN	no
7	42	entrepreneur	divorced	tertiary	yes	2	yes	no	NaN	5	may	380	1	-1	0	NaN	no
8	58	retired	married	primary	no	121	yes	no	NaN	5	may	50	1	-1	0	NaN	no
9	43	technician	single	secondary	no	593	yes	no	NaN	5	may	55	1	-1	0	NaN	no

Figure 6.8: A screenshot showing the first 10 instances of the dataset

The missing values are shown as **NaN**, as explained previously.

3. Select the metric that's the most appropriate for measuring the performance of the model, considering that the purpose of the study is to detect clients who would subscribe to the term deposit.

   The metric to evaluate the performance of the model is the **precision** metric, as it compares the correctly classified positive labels against the total number of instances predicted as positive.

4. Pre-process the dataset.

   The process of handling missing values is handled as per the concepts we learned about in *Chapter 1, Introduction to Scikit-Learn*, and that have been applied throughout this book. Use the following code to check for missing values:

   ```
   data.isnull().sum()
   ```

   Based on the results, you will observe that only four features contain missing values: **job** (288), **education** (1,857), **contact** (13,020), and **poutcome** (36,959).

The first two features can be left unhandled, considering that the missing values represent less than 5% of the entire data. On the other hand, 28.8% of the values are missing from the **contact** feature, and taking into account that the feature refers to the mode of contact, which is considered to be irrelevant for determining whether a person will subscribe to a new product, it is safe to remove this feature from the study. Finally, the **poutcome** feature is missing 81.7% of its values, which is why this feature is also removed from the study.

Using the following code, the preceding two features are dropped:

```
data = data.drop(["contact", "poutcome"], axis=1)
```

As we explained in *Chapter 1, Introduction to Scikit-Learn*, and applied throughout this book, the process of converting categorical features into their numeric form is as follows.

For all nominal features, use the following code:

```
enc = LabelEncoder()
features_to_convert=["job","marital","default",\
                     "housing","loan","month","y"]
for i in features_to_convert:
    data[i] = enc.fit_transform(data[i].astype('str'))
```

The preceding code, as explained in previous chapters, converts all the qualitative features into their numeric forms.

Next, to handle the ordinal feature, we must use the following code, as mentioned in *Step 4*:

```
data['education'] = data['education'].fillna('unknown')
encoder = ['unknown','primary','secondary','tertiary']

for i, word in enumerate(encoder):
    data['education'] = data['education'].astype('str').\
                        str.replace(word, str(i))
data['education'] = data['education'].astype('int64')
data.head()
```

Here, the first line converts **NaN** values into the word **unknown**, while the second line sets the order of the values in the feature. Next, a **for** loop is used to replace each word with a number that follows an order. For the preceding example, **0** will be used to replace the word **unknown**, then **1** will be used instead of **primary**, and so on. Finally, the whole column is converted into an integer type since the **replace** function writes down the numbers as strings.

If we display the head of the resulting DataFrame, the output is as follows:

	age	job	marital	education	default	balance	housing	loan	day	month	duration	campaign	pdays	previous	y
0	58	4	1	3	0	2143	1	0	5	8	261	1	-1	0	0
1	44	10	2	2	0	29	1	0	5	8	151	1	-1	0	0
2	33	2	1	2	0	2	1	1	5	8	76	1	-1	0	0
3	47	1	1	0	0	1506	1	0	5	8	92	1	-1	0	0
4	33	5	2	0	0	1	0	0	5	8	198	1	-1	0	0

Figure 6.9: A screenshot showing the first five instances of the dataset after converting the categorical features into numerical ones

We learned how to deal with the outliers in *Chapter 1, Introduction to Scikit-Learn*. Use the following code to check for outliers:

```
outliers = {}

for i in range(data.shape[1]):
    min_t = data[data.columns[i]].mean() \
            - (3 * data[data.columns[i]].std())
    max_t = data[data.columns[i]].mean() \
            + (3 * data[data.columns[i]].std())
    count = 0

    for j in data[data.columns[i]]:
        if j < min_t or j > max_t:
            count += 1
    outliers[data.columns[i]] = [count, data.shape[0]]

print(outliers)
```

If we print the resulting dictionary, we get the following output:

```
{'age': [381, 45211], 'job': [0, 45211], 'marital': [0, 45211],
'education': [0, 45211], 'default': [815, 45211], 'balance': [745,
45211], 'housing': [0, 45211], 'loan': [0, 45211], 'day': [0, 45211],
'month': [0, 45211], 'duration': [963, 45211], 'campaign': [840,
45211], 'pdays': [1723, 45211], 'previous': [582, 45211], 'y': [0,
45211]}
```

As we can see, the outliers do not account for more than 5% of the total values in each feature, which is why they can be left unhandled.

This can be verified by taking the feature with the most outliers (**pdays**) and dividing the number of outliers by the total number of instances (1,723 divided by 45,211). The result from that operation is 0.038, which is equivalent to 3.8%. This means that the feature only has 3.8% of the outlier values.

5. Separate the features from the class label and split the dataset into three sets (training, validation, and testing).

    To separate the features from the target value, use the following code:

    ```
    X = data.drop("y", axis = 1)
    Y = data["y"]
    ```

    Next, to perform a 60/20/20 split, use the following code:

    ```
    X_new, X_test, \
    Y_new, Y_test = train_test_split(X, Y, test_size=0.2,\
                                     random_state = 0)
    test_size = X_test.shape[0] / X_new.shape[0]
    X_train, X_dev, \
    Y_train, Y_dev = train_test_split(X_new, Y_new, \
                                      test_size=test_size,\
                                      random_state = 0)
    print(X_train.shape, Y_train.shape, X_dev.shape, \
        Y_dev.shape, X_test.shape, Y_test.shape)
    ```

    If we print the shape of all the subsets, the output is as follows:

    ```
    (27125, 14) (27125,) (9043, 14) (9043,) (9043, 14) (9043,)
    ```

6. Use the decision tree algorithm on the dataset and train the model:

    ```
    model_tree = DecisionTreeClassifier(random_state = 2)
    model_tree.fit(X_train, Y_train)
    ```

> **NOTE**
>
> As a reminder, the output from calling the `fit` method consists of the model currently being trained with all the parameters that it takes in.

7. Use the multilayer perceptron algorithm on the dataset and train the model. To revisit this, go to *Chapter 5, Artificial Neural Networks: Predicting Annual Income*:

```
model_NN = MLPClassifier(random_state = 2)
model_NN.fit(X_train, Y_train)
```

8. Evaluate both models by using the metric that was selected previously.

    Using the following code, it is possible to measure the precision score of the decision tree model:

```
X_sets = [X_train, X_dev, X_test]
Y_sets = [Y_train, Y_dev, Y_test]

precision = []

for i in range(0, len(X_sets)):
    pred = model_tree.predict(X_sets[i])
    score = precision_score(Y_sets[i], pred)
    precision.append(score)

print(precision)
```

If we print the list containing the precision score for each of the sets for the decision tree model, the output is as follows:

```
[1.0, 0.43909348441926344, 0.4208059981255858]
```

The same code can be modified to calculate the score for the multilayer perceptron:

```
X_sets = [X_train, X_dev, X_test]
Y_sets = [Y_train, Y_dev, Y_test]

precision = []
```

```
for i in range(0, len(X_sets)):
    pred = model_NN.predict(X_sets[i])
    score = precision_score(Y_sets[i], pred)
    precision.append(score)

print(precision)
```

If we print the list containing the precision score for each of the sets for the multilayer perceptron model, the output is as follows:

```
[0.35577647236029525, 0.35199283475145543, 0.3470483005366726]
```

The precision score for all subsets of data for both models is shown in the following table:

	Decision Tree	Multilayer Perception
Training sets	1.00	0.35
Validation sets	0.44	0.35
Testing sets	0.42	0.35

Figure 6.10: Precision scores for both models

9. Fine-tune some of the hyperparameters to fix the issues that were detected during the evaluation of the model by performing error analysis.

Although the precision of the decision tree on the training sets is perfect, on comparing it against the results of the other two sets, it is possible to conclude that the model suffers from high variance.

On the other hand, the multilayer perceptron has a similar performance on all three sets, but the overall performance is low, which means that the model is more likely to be suffering from high bias.

Considering this, for the decision tree model, both the minimum number of samples required to be at a leaf node and the maximum depth of the tree are changed in order to simplify the model. On the other hand, for the multilayer perceptron, the number of iterations, the number of hidden layers, the number of units in each layer, and the tolerance for optimization are changed.

The following code shows the final values that were used for the hyperparameters of the decision tree algorithm, considering that to arrive at them it is required to try different values:

```
model_tree = DecisionTreeClassifier(random_state = 2, \
                                    min_samples_leaf=100, \
                                    max_depth=100)
model_tree.fit(X_train, Y_train)
```

The following snippet displays the final values used for the hyperparameters of the multilayer perceptron algorithm:

```
model_NN = \
    MLPClassifier(random_state = 2, max_iter=1000,\
                  hidden_layer_sizes = [100,100,50,25,25], \
                  tol=1e-4)
model_NN.fit(X_train, Y_train)
```

> **NOTE**
>
> As a reminder, the output from calling the **fit** method consists of the model currently being trained with all the parameters that it takes in.

10. Compare the final versions of your models and select the one that you consider best fits the data.

Using the same code as in previous steps, it is possible to calculate the precision of the decision tree model over the different sets of data:

```
X_sets = [X_train, X_dev, X_test]
Y_sets = [Y_train, Y_dev, Y_test]

precision = []

for i in range(0, len(X_sets)):
    pred = model_tree.predict(X_sets[i])
    score = precision_score(Y_sets[i], pred)
    precision.append(score)

print(precision)
```

The output list should look as follows:

```
[0.6073670992046881, 0.5691158156911582, 0.5448113207547169]
```

To calculate the precision of the multilayer perceptron, the following code snippet can be used:

```
X_sets = [X_train, X_dev, X_test]
Y_sets = [Y_train, Y_dev, Y_test]

precision = []

for i in range(0, len(X_sets)):
    pred = model_NN.predict(X_sets[i])
    score = precision_score(Y_sets[i], pred)
    precision.append(score)

print(precision)
```

The resulting list should look as follows:

```
[0.759941089837997, 0.5920398009950248, 0.5509259259259259]
```

By calculating the precision score for all three sets for the newly trained models, we obtain the following values:

	Decision Tree	Multilayer Perception
Training sets	0.61	0.76
Validation sets	0.57	0.60
Testing sets	0.54	0.55

Figure 6.11: Precision scores for the newly trained models

NOTE

To access the source code for this specific section, please refer to https://packt.live/2Rplhn9.

This section does not currently have an online interactive example, and will need to be run locally.

An improvement in performance for both models is achieved, and by comparing the values, it is possible to conclude that the multilayer perceptron outperforms the decision tree model. Based on this, the multilayer perceptron is selected as the better model for solving the data problem.

> **NOTE**
>
> You are encouraged to continue to fine-tune the parameters to reach an even higher precision score.

ACTIVITY 6.02: SAVING AND LOADING THE FINAL MODEL FOR THE BANK MARKETING DATASET

Solution:

1. Open the Jupyter Notebook from *Activity 6.01, Performing the Preparation and Creation Stages for the Bank Marketing Dataset*.

2. For learning purposes, take the model that you selected as the best model, remove the **random_state** argument, and run it a couple of times.

3. Save the model that you choose as the best performing one into a file named **final_model.pkl**.

> **NOTE**
>
> The model selected in this book is the multilayer perceptron, which uses a **random_state** of **2**, was trained for 1,000 iterations with five hidden layers of size 100, 100, 50, 25 and 25, and a tolerance level of 1e-4.

The code for this is as follows:

```
path = os.getcwd() + "/final_model.pkl"
file = open(path, "wb")
pickle.dump(model_NN, file)
```

4. Open a new Jupyter Notebook and import the required modules and class:

```
from sklearn.neural_network import MLPClassifier
import pickle
import os
```

5. Load the saved model:

```
path = os.getcwd() + "/final_model.pkl"
file = open(path, "rb")
model = pickle.load(file)
```

6. Perform a prediction for an individual by using the following values: **42, 2, 0, 0, 1, 2, 1, 0, 5, 8, 380, 1, –1, 0**:

```
pred = model.predict([[42,2,0,0,1,2,1,0,5,8,380,1,-1,0]])
print(pred)
```

> **NOTE**
>
> To access the source code for this specific section, please refer to
> https://packt.live/2UIWFss.
>
> This section does not currently have an online interactive example, and will
> need to be run locally.

If we printing the **pred** variable, the output is **0**, which is the numeric form of **No**. This means that the individual is more likely to not subscribe to the new product.

ACTIVITY 6.03: ALLOWING INTERACTION WITH THE BANK MARKETING DATASET MODEL

Solution:

1. In a text editor, create a class object that contains two main functions. One should be an initializer that loads the saved model, while the other should be a **predict** method where the data is fed to the model to retrieve an output:

```
import pickle
import os
```

As per the preceding snippet, the first step is to import all the required elements to locate the saved model and deserialize it:

```
Class NN_Model(object):

    def __init__(self):
        path = os.getcwd() + "/model_exercise.pkl"
        file = open(path, "rb")
        self.model = pickle.load(file)

    def predict(self, age, job, marital, education, \
                default, balance, housing, loan, day, \
                month, duration, campaign, pdays, previous):
        X = [[age, job, marital, education, default, \
             balance, housing, loan, day, month, \
             duration, campaign, pdays, previous]]
        return self.model.predict(X)
```

Next, as per the preceding code snippet, the class that will connect the saved model with the channel of interaction is programmed. It should have an initializer method to deserialize and load the saved model, and a **predict** method to feed the input data to the model to perform a prediction.

2. In a Jupyter Notebook, import and initialize the class that you created in the previous step. Next, create the variables that will hold the values for the features of a new observation and use the following values: **42, 2, 0, 0, 1, 2, 1, 0, 5, 8, 380, 1, –1, 0**:

```
from trainedModel import NN_Model

model = NN_Model()

age = 42
job = 2
marital = 0
education = 0
default = 1
```

```
balance = 2
housing = 1
loan = 0
day = 5
month = 8
duration = 380
campaign = 1
pdays = -1
previous = 0
```

Perform a prediction by applying the **predict** method:

```
pred = model.predict(age=age, job=job, marital=marital, \
                     education=education, default=default, \
                     balance=balance, housing=housing, \
                     loan=loan, day=day, month=month, \
                     duration=duration, campaign=campaign, \
                     pdays=pdays, previous=previous)
print(pred)
```

By printing the variable, the prediction is equal to **0**; that is, the individual with the given features is not likely to subscribe to the product, as can be seen here:

```
[0]
```

> **NOTE**
>
> To access the source code for this specific section, please refer to https://packt.live/2Y2yBCJ.
>
> You can also run this example online at https://packt.live/3d6ku3E. You must execute the entire Notebook in order to get the desired result.

Throughout the activities in this chapter, you have successfully learned how to develop a complete machine learning solution, going from data pre-processing and training the model to selecting the best performing model using error analysis and saving the model to be able to make use of it effectively.

INDEX

CPSIA information can be obtained
at www.ICGtesting.com
Printed in the USA
BVHW010808290820
587582BV00008B/810